Samuel T. Francis

Samuel T. Francis
and Revolution from the Middle

Joseph Scotchie

Samuel T. Francis and Revolution from the Middle
Copyright© 2025 by Joseph Scotchie

ALL RIGHTS RESERVED. No part of this publication may be reproduced, distributed, or transmitted in any form or by any means, including photocopying, recording, or other electronic or mechanical methods, or by any information storage and retrieval system without the prior written permission of the publisher, except in the case of very brief quotations embodied in critical reviews and certain other non-commercial uses permitted by copyright law.

Produced in the Republic of South Carolina by

SHOTWELL PUBLISHING LLC
Post Office Box 2592
Columbia, So. Carolina 29202
www.ShotwellPublishing.com

Cover: Sam Francis Portrait, courtesy of *Chronicles* Magazine.

ISBN: 978-1-963506-29-7

FIRST EDITION

10 9 8 7 6 5 4 3 2

Contents

Introduction vii
1. Our Man in Swampville 1
2. Allies 5
3. High Hopes 19
4. Burnhamite 35
5. Beautiful Losers 53
6. America First 69
7. A Populist Revolution? 85
8. Purged 95
9. Conservative Wars 113
10. Explicit 123
11. A Pep Talk for Western Man 135
12. Anarcho-Tyranny: America Surrendered 145
13. A Prophet Is Proved Right 163
14. Francis At Rest 173
Notes 183
Acknowledgments 187
Bibliography 189
Index 195
About the Author 201

Samuel T. Francis on America, foreseeing the Trump revolution from the middle:

> What we have in this country is both anarchy (the failure of the state to enforce the laws) and, at the same time, tyranny—the enforcement of laws by the state for oppressive purposes; the criminalization of the law-abiding and innocent through exorbitant taxation, bureaucratic regulation, the invasion of privacy, and the engineering of social institutions, such as the family and local schools; the imposition of thought control through "sensitivity training" and multiculturalist curricula, "hate crime" laws, gun-control laws that punish or disarm otherwise law-abiding citizens but have no impact on violent criminals, who get guns illegally, and a vast labyrinth of other measures. In a word, *anarcho-tyranny*.

Introduction

SAMUEL T. FRANCIS (1947-2005) was the most provocative and prophetic political commentator of his time.

A native of Chatttanooga, Tennessee, with familial roots in both the Revolutionary War and the Civil War, Francis was a graduate of Johns Hopkins University. He hit his stride at the University of North Carolina where he pursued a Ph.D. in English history.

Next came work at the Heritage Foundation, the office of Senator John P. East (R—NC), and, most significantly, as an editorial writer for the *Washington Times*. During the 1980s, Sam Francis was a typical Cold War conservative. He continued his prodigious reading and writing projects, becoming a disciple of James Burnham, critic of a managerial state designed to manipulate the minds and actions of the masses and of M.E. Bradford, a fifth generation Texan and a premiere scholar on the Founding Era.

With the end of the Cold War, Francis solidified his worldview. Along with Thomas Fleming, editor of *Chronicles,* and his new ally, Patrick J. Buchanan, he became the penman of an emerging America First platform: no to unnecessary wars, free trade, and mass immigration; yes to traditional Christian morality and an unapologetic defense of American and Western culture and history.

Banished from the precincts of respectable conservatism, Francis became more radical, seeking to create a white racial consciousness among those Middle American Radicals who elected Richard Nixon and Ronald Reagan to landslide victories.

Sam Francis sought to analyze and celebrate the achievements of Western man throughout the centuries. On a poignant note, he became the voice of those lonely Americans who were alarmed at going to the shopping mall and not seeing any familiar faces.

Notably, Francis created the concept of Anarcho-Tyranny to describe the American government regime of his time. It identifies an authoritarian elite that oppressively regulates its citizens but is unwilling to protect their interests and caters to the lawless lower classes. The term is still in use, even by some who don't know its origin, and has been widely discussed.

In response to such an elite, Sam Francis favored an uprising of the middle elements of society to create a new regime. It can fairly be said that he advocated and anticipated Donald Trump's victory in the 2024 presidential election, two decades before it happened.

1.

Our Man in Swampville

AT UNC, SAM FRANCIS met Clyde Wilson, a lifetime friend. Francis, a graduate student in History, was slightly acquainted with Tom Fleming, a graduate student in Classics. Later, Fleming, as editor of *Chronicles*, greatly promoted Francis's stature and prominence as a writer. The liberal university was the seed of an important conservative intellectual movement. The young Francis would have to make a living. Writing and publishing would become his life's vocation. No matter what he did for a living, Sam was primarily a writer, forever juggling such projects as reviews, essays, columns, speeches, and book-length manuscripts.

Samuel Todd Francis was a public intellectual. He was also a private man. He lived his adult life in the Washington area. Francis lived the normal life of a 20th century American commuter: driving, first from his home in Maryland to offices in the District of Columbia, and later to a workspace on Oronoco Street in Alexandria, Virginia, that fittingly enough was in the boyhood home of Robert E. Lee. Prolific in all ways, Francis was a policy analyst, speechwriter, author, essayist, columnist, editor, and a public speaker. For millions convinced of America's decline, Sam Francis was *the* voice of white despair.

In the 1990s, he gained fame as an intellectual force behind his friend Patrick J. Buchanan's presidential campaigns. No memoirist, Sam Francis rarely wrote about himself. His 1995 firing from the *Washington Times* was a news story. Francis, however, stayed out of the limelight. He called off any demonstrations planned on his behalf and refused media interviews. He saved his account of the firing for two essays in his *Chronicles* column.

Inspired by, among others, Russell Kirk, Murray Rothbard, and M.E. Bradford, plus the towering example of Thomas Fleming, the paleoconservatism of the 1990s and beyond was determined to be proficient in all things Western. Their arguments were based on a thorough reading of Western literature, philosophy, theology, and history. Sam's worldview was formed by such conservative thinkers as Bradford, James Burnham, and Willmoore Kendall. Later influences included the sociologist Donald E. Warren, prophet of the Middle American Radicals (MARS), and Patrick Buchanan, supplemented by such European leftists as Antonio Gramsci, writers who maintained that a cultural revolution must precede real political results.

Sam Francis was not famous or wealthy or a television celebrity. Friends fondly remembered his wit, humor and learning, his abilities as a ballroom dancer, a moviegoer, a marksman, and a world-class conversationalist. Francis lived a life of the mind. An eager student of Western culture, he could dazzle friends, colleagues, and audiences with his wide scope. As Jared Taylor recalled:

> As with so many men of great talent, Sam's brilliance was just as striking in areas for which he was not well known. He read deeply in literature. He had an encyclopedic knowledge of the author H.P. Lovecraft, on whom he wrote several essays. If I managed to find the time to read a novel by Joseph Conrad or a poem by Alexander Pope, Sam always had insightful recollections about the author and the work itself.

And not just literature. For Taylor, Francis was a born historian:

> Unlike many people, whose Ph.D. is a labor undertaken for professional purposes and quickly left

behind, Sam's historical learning reflected a real joy in knowing the past. He seemed to retain all he had ever learned and was an inexhaustible source of insight and information. When I might stumble across an obscure but piquant incident from a 19th century British colonial campaign, Sam would know everything about the campaign, why the colonial minister had ordered it, and what objections had been raised by the foreign minister. When I first became acquainted with the Greek historian and geographer Strabo, Sam, of course, knew all about him and why he was important.

Francis read for enjoyment. His Maryland home held a large personal library. Those reading marathons shaped his thinking.

After his firing from the *Washington Times* Francis persevered. In his lifetime, Sam published numerous books and monographs: *The Soviet Strategy of Terror; Power and History: The Political Thought of James Burnham; Beautiful Losers: Essays on the Failure of American Conservatism; Revolution from the Middle;* and *America Extinguished: Mass Immigration and the Disintegration of American Culture.* After his death, friends edited other collections: *Essential Writings on Race, Shots Fired,* and *Ethno-Politics.* A bulky manuscript, *Leviathan and Its Enemies,* was discovered and prepared for a 2018 publication.

Sam Francis's words burn in memory. They burn on the printed page. Through learning, courage, and perseverance, he evolved from a movement conservative to one of the great and unique minds of late 20th and early 21st century life.

The 21st century is here. The government engages in endless wars abroad. The southern border is open. College campuses are rife with students chanting anti-American slogans. Crimes of all sorts take place in broad daylight. Figures in American history once revered—Christopher Columbus, George Washington, Thomas

Jefferson, Andrew Jackson, Robert E. Lee, Theodore Roosevelt, Woodrow Wilson—are now reviled. Statues and monuments are vandalized, removed, and sometimes destroyed. Up to 70 percent of Americans declare the nation to be on the wrong track.

Samuel Francis was a thinker who warned of the decline of America and its Western heritage. The failure of respectable conservatism, which he firmly pointed out, left a regime where "invade the world, invite the world" seemed inevitable. However, the vigorous Trump populist movement of 2024 can be seen as the Revolution from the Middle that Francis prophetically proposed and advocated.

2.

Allies

THE BAYLOR SCHOOL is a private institution in Chattanooga, Tennessee. On its website it lists a string of distinguished graduates. The list is impressive. It includes two mayors of that city, novelists (Catherine Lacey, Andrew Golden), prominent journalists (Allan Murray of the *Wall Street Journal*, Thomas Jolley of the *New York Times*), a musical director of New York City's famed Radio City Music Hall (Donald Pippin), plus an array of businessmen, physicians, and educators.

Sam Francis's name does not appear among them. He was a 1965 graduate of that school. Francis went on to a distinguished career, helping to create a revival of America First as a force in American politics. The controversy along the way was enormous. In death, his influence and legacy live on. As do the controversies surrounding his worldview and the blunt but scholarly way in which he presented it. His alma mater would not dare mention his existence, much less his achievements. It isn't worth the controversy. A private institution, the Baylor School hardly needs the overwhelmingly negative publicity that would come from such an association.

And so, Sam Francis's notoriety in a paragraph. American conservatism from the New Deal onward has been a mostly irrelevant footnote in American history. Its thinkers have been plenty bold, but without a political party unable to make a dent in a liberal nation. That, too, is Sam Francis's fate. He did, however, leave behind an eye-opening body of work, one that is more alive than ever.

Sam Francis's surviving older sister can trace the family's maternal ancestors, a clan that emigrated from England to North America sometime in the 17th century. At first, the Cate family settled in North Carolina. In the early 1800s, the homestead moved to Tennessee. Joseph Charles Cate was a veteran of the Revolutionary War. His land grant was for a large farm in Niota, Tennessee, one dubbed Big Springs Farm. That land was anchored by a brick home that was constructed from 1823 to 1827.

A later Cate male descendant fought for the Confederate side during the Civil War. As a young woman, Sam Francis's grandmother married Samuel H. Ford. The latter moved to Chattanooga and practiced law until his death at age 90 in 1960. According to Clyde Wilson, the young Sam Francis was especially close to the grandfather that he was named after.

The Ford's had only one daughter from their marriage. Sam's mother, Julia, married Todd Ware Francis in 1938. A daughter, also named Julia, was born later that year. Samuel Todd Francis was born in 1947.

There is a more famous family connection. When Sam Dickson, among others, attended Sam's funeral in 2005, he entered through the back door residence of Julia Irwin, the man's older sister's house in Lookout Mountain, Tennessee. On the wall of the kitchen was a portrait of a woman familiar to most students of American history. Dickson and others thought the portrait looked familiar. It was. When asked, Mrs. Irwin surprised the guests. "That's Mary Todd Lincoln," she announced. Yes, the First Lady of the United States during the Civil War was Sam's distant relative on his maternal side of the family. Throughout his life, Sam never bothered mentioning this. He was a son of the American Revolution and of the Confederacy.

Along with Julia, Sam grew up in Chattanooga during the boom years of the 1950s and '60s. A gifted student, Sam, according to family legend, often helped his older sister with her homework. When he was only four, a dentist caught Sam studying a book in the waiting room. The dentist thought the youngster was trying to memorize it. Not the case, family members replied. The boy had already taught himself to read and was enjoying a new text. As a youngster, he won awards for student achievement. In high school, Sam displayed traces of literary brilliance. All teenagers write poetry. Sam's efforts were predictably innocent, including a hymn to a local gardener.

Apostrophe to a Gardener

Your garden has grown. In its youth
Its colors were rose and tulip, like unto
The early bursting of the sun in early spring,
The early twilight of late October,
When frosty sunlight silverplates the hills
And makes the clouds like shining stock-cars racing.
Rainbows that spat into a blind man's eye
Were in your garden, but it has grown old.
So now its dry stalks haunt the dust,
Specters of the tulip and the rose, and toads
And grasshoppers chortle in their brown dead mold.
Burnt sticks, where flowers grew, now cringe
Beneath the winter sun.
Sand and grit, where the black loam breathed,
Now dance in shapeless jig
To a raving wind.
Your egos were too much for it. They could
Not stand to see much green and spangled youth,

And so they scorched it down beneath
The frozen glare of torches, red, all red, against
The summer night of stars, bubbling open,
Red with hate and twisting ignorance,
Yet they lit fires that kept you warm
That summer night (cold in summer, cold in night),
Yet they set a passion in yourself
That tore your heart and mind apart, and yet,
They kept you warm that night (cold in summer).
Cold in night, cold with all the loneliness
Of a thousand crimson Eyes.

Not bad for a 17-year-old. This verse, which won a literary prize at the Baylor School, showed traces of key elements in his later prose work. There is humour: how dramatic can a gardener's profession be? The reference to stock car racing reflects Sam's Southern upbringing as that sport, with Richard Petty at the helm, achieved soaring success in the sports-crazy 1960s. There is a harder edge, too, nothing dramatic, but the line "Your egos were too much for it" foreshadows the blunt language Francis would make as his trademark. That wasn't all. As an adolescent, Francis displayed flashes of the humour that would make him notable. Students at the Baylor School voted him "the wittiest" in the 1965 graduating class.

After graduating from the Baylor School, Sam Francis entered Johns Hopkins University in Baltimore. Family members recall him being excited at the news of acceptance. One of the premier liberal arts universities on the East Coast, Johns Hopkins was founded in 1876 by the American entrepreneur of that same name. Johns Hopkins has its own famous alumni, including Woodrow Wilson, Spiro Agnew, John Dewey, Rachel Carson, Madeline Albright, Michael Bloomberg, plus the dubious Alger Hiss. Sidney Lanier had been on the faculty. As an undergraduate, Sam continued his ambitious reading projects. He would graduate in 1969 with a B.A. in History.

Inspired by the works of Charles Dickens, Alexander Pope, and H.P. Lovecraft, among others, Francis pursued graduate school studies in English history. His destination? The University of North Carolina at Chapel Hill. The choice proved decisive. There, Sam met friends for life. The early Seventies was the heyday of Richard Nixon's Silent Majority. Chapel Hill, as with all liberal arts universities, was decidedly leftist, its student body leaders even inviting Jane Fonda on campus for a talk. Francis was not a youthful liberal turned conservative. As with his later friend, Pat Buchanan, Sam was "right from the beginning." At Chapel Hill he found like-minded soulmates, among them students E. Christian Kopff and Clyde Wilson.

A handful of them, Sam Francis included, wanted to form a conservative debate and discussion society. The required faculty sponsor was John Shelton Reed, a young sociologist who would publish numerous books on Southern culture. He was preceded by libertarian economics professor Clarence Philbrook. UNC decreed that any student group with "Carolina" in their name sign a non-discrimination pledge. Iconoclastic from the start, Sam and his friends refused. Members puckishly renamed the Carolina Conservative Club to be the Orange County Anti-Jacobin League.

To complement Sam's budding worldview, an important addition was Clyde Wilson. Wilson had worked in journalism before enrolling in Chapel Hill. In the early 1970s, Wilson was married with a young family as he pursued a Ph.D. in history. He had also been published in both *Modern Age* and *National Review*. Sam Francis called Wilson and asked him, as the most "prominent" conservative on the liberal campus, to join the club. Wilson attended a meeting. It was a decision he never regretted.

The "League" made no big impression. Still, some of its members bonded for life. "I had a full-time job and a family and was trying to get a doctorate in History, so I did not have much time," Wilson remembered decades later. "But I went and it was a major thing in my life. We met and discussed readings like [James] Burnham, [Richard] Weaver, and others. There were at various times half a dozen to a dozen people. The main people were Sam, myself, and Chris Kopff. After discussion we adjourned to a redneck bar for a hamburger and beer."

In 1989, when Walker Percy won the Rockford Institute's annual T.S. Eliot Award for Scholarly Letters, he was introduced to the *Chronicles'* editorial staff by Thomas Fleming, then making his mark as the magazine's editor. As greetings were exchanged, Percy, himself a graduate of Chapel Hill, asked, "My God, Tom, what are you running here, a Tar Heel conspiracy?"

The purpose of such clubs as the Orange County Anti-Jacobin League is not just good talk among friends, young men exchanging ideas. It is also a way to make allies for life and with it career connections. Sam thought for himself, but he was not a loner. Aware of his standing as a hard right conservative in the world of John Hopkins-University of North Carolina-New South liberalism, Sam valued allies, especially ones that were already published. His immense reading habits continued.

Throughout the 1960s and '70s, William F. Buckley, Jr.'s *National Review* remained the publication that budding conservatives would bite their teeth on. In addition to Buckley, *NR*'s most venerable editor was James Burnham, author of the bi-weekly column, "The Third World War." Sam admired the old *National Review* crew: Frank Meyer, Willmoore Kendall, James J. Kilpatrick, and such non-masthead contributors as Kirk and Weaver. Burnham proved to be his favorite. Through such works as *The Managerial Revolution* and *The Machiavellians*, Sam would learn from Burnham that lust for power prevailed in the hearts of men. All the learning in the world counted for nothing without political might behind it.

Francis graduated from Chapel Hill with a Ph.D. in English history. During that time, he spent a semester living in England while completing the dissertation. Great men never lack for admiration or friendship. Sam was no different. To his legion of readers, he was a faithful correspondent (the author included). At meetings of the John Randolph Club, the Council of Conservative Citizens, or American Renaissance, Francis was always the center of attention—fans flocked around him after a session of speeches and conferences ended. Sam's readers were the man's friends. I recall the reception he received while entering the Soldiers and Sailors Club in New York City for a spring 1999 weekday evening talk. Sam received a standing ovation as soon as he arrived. "This is like Diana," he joked, referring to the recent outpouring of emotion given to the Princess of Wales following her death in an automobile accident.

Being a conservative in the five boroughs is a waste: How many decades can a man bang his head against a wall? The ovation was as much a sigh of relief as in appreciation. *"Voila!* He has arrived! Somebody's who's on *our* side!"

Throughout his 30-year career, Francis revolved in a dynamic circle of provocative thinkers and writers. This involved such respectable outlets and figures as the Heritage Foundation, the *Washington Times*, and the offices of Senators John East (R—NC), Jesse Helms (R—NC), and Jeremiah Denton (R—AL). And, most importantly, the circle of famous pundit Pat Buchanan. Away from journalism and politics, his colleagues included not just Fleming and Bradford, but also Wilson, Paul Gottfried, Chilton Williamson, Jr., and Murray Rothbard, the great libertarian.

After being banished from the precincts of respectability, Sam found new allies, among them Joseph Sobran and Jared Taylor. Sam moved from respectable right to far right out of conviction. Conservatism, as understood from the mid-1950s to 1988, was a failure. Time to go radical—and explicit. This stand gained Sam an unwavering nationwide following, people who stood with him when he faced public humiliation at the hands of his superiors at the *Washington Times* and from "Conservatism, Inc."

Samuel T. Francis and Revolution from the Middle

In 1980, the story of postwar conservatism turned on a dime, from the irrelevancy of old ladies in sneakers to the glory of Ronald Reagan and the fall of the Berlin Wall. Decades after Reagan retired, conservatives still lived off the fumes of the Roaring Eighties. The careers of William F. Buckley, Jr. and George F. Will were bathed in triumph. No glory in the Sam Francis story. Instead, frustration and bewilderment, saved by the man's humour and the knowledge that by going hard right he had made the correct choice. With the triumph of multiculturalism and political correctness, Sam stood his ground, refusing to budge an inch, i.e., by saying something positive about Franklin D. Roosevelt, John F. Kennedy, or Lyndon Johnson.

A controversial column or even a single sentence, phrase, or word cost him greatly. The mainstream publications that carried his byline before dropping it included not only the *Washington Times* and its sister glossy magazine supplement, *The World & I,* but also *National Review, Human Events,* and *The New American.* Cuts in salary, lost jobs, lost platforms, worries about even making a living, haunted Sam's professional life.

According to such friends as Chilton Williamson, Jr. and Scott McConnell, Francis was puzzled by his banishment. After Sam's untimely death in 2005, Williamson maintained that his friend's most controversial belief: that Western civilization was the product of European peoples and that it could not survive the defeat of such peoples was merely empirical. Why the uproar? Had not conservatives, prior to the 1980s, said such things repeatedly? In the late Nineties, the Randolph Club held a conference in London. During a break, McConnell recalled seeing Sam alone in thought, sitting on a park bench. "What's wrong, Sam?" McConnell ventured. "Nothing," Francis replied. "I was just wondering what happened to my career."

In his entry on Francis in the much-publicized *American Conservatism: An Encyclopedia,* John Zmirak proclaimed:

For asserting that European Americans, as much as Asian, African, and Hispanic Americans, had right to view themselves as a cohesive group with identifiable interests, Francis found himself marginalized and increasingly opposed to a conservative movement that sought to ground its polemics not in the defense of Western, Christian culture, but in the Enlightenment ideology of America's most prominent founders.

Why blame Sam Francis? His views on race and culture were similar to ones made during modern conservatism's early years. Plus, there are the famous dog whistles. As election time approached, Barry Goldwater, Richard Nixon, Ronald Reagan, George H.W. Bush, and, most unapologetically, Donald J. Trump all went pell-mell after white voters, taking right wing views on civil rights, crime, busing, welfare, and immigration. Francis, as we shall see, was most explicit. It was no accident.

Where Sam Francis parted company with respectable official conservatives was his interpretation of both American and Western history. Francis did not view the West as something universal. Its culture could not be transported to other nations using force or by the wisdom of Hollywood movies and the annual Super Bowl telecast. American foreign policy should exist for the benefit of its own people.

The West, he maintained, was something concrete: a certain people with certain attributes and characteristics, a people apart. No wars for democracy. No immigration from non-Western nations, a trade policy that keeps jobs at home, a foreign policy that keeps the troops alive. As much as his friend Pat Buchanan, Sam Francis was robustly America First. His insistence on the United States as a Western, Christian nation with an Anglo-Saxon Protestant core repulsed his one-time allies on the respectable right.

Thomas Fleming, too, attended Chapel Hill in the early 1970s, pursuing his own Ph.D. in the classics. Fleming was friends with Kopff, a fellow classicist-in-training. By the end of the decade,

Fleming, who had launched a career in academia, had moved back to South Carolina and wanted to start a journal of opinion defending and celebrating Southern culture and history. Kopff, at long distance in Colorado, arranged for a meeting between Fleming and Wilson. A lifelong bond was joined. When *Southern Partisan* ran its inaugural issue in 1979, Fleming and Wilson were the co-editors. Through his friendship with Wilson, Sam Francis, then employed at the Heritage Foundation, became part of the inner circle, contributing his own column to this risky adventure.

Sam entered the orbit of America's most original and provocative editor—and a great essayist to boot. Fleming was a friend for life. As important, Fleming, as editor of *Chronicles*, proved to be an implacable ally, never faltering in his loyalty to his friend. Fleming took a circular route to his destination as the editorial founder of paleoconservatism. Born in 1945 in Milwaukee, Wisconsin, Fleming moved with his family, first to Florida and later to Charleston, South Carolina, where the senior Fleming owned a minor league baseball team affiliated with the Chicago White Sox. Charleston made Fleming. The Southland's legendary "eternal city," Charleston prided itself on its classical heritage, complete with stunning architecture and a tradition of classical education.

Fleming, too, was an outstanding student. During his senior year of high school, he became so bored with schoolwork that he dropped out before earning a diploma. No matter. Harvard University offered Fleming a full scholarship if (if only!) he would go back to high school and complete his studies. Fleming said no. Decades later, he never regretted his decision, claiming that if he had gone to Harvard, his career would be as a mere *apparatchik* in the entirely ineffectual conservative movement rather than that of a ground-breaking editor.

Fleming struck pay dirt at home, enrolling in nearby College of Charleston, an institution renowned for its classical studies. With Charleston and the classics, Fleming had found a home. The young man enjoyed staking out a park bench near the now destroyed Calhoun monument and pouring his way through the literature and history of Athens and Rome. Chapel Hill was Fleming's next stop. UNC was considered to be one of the top classical departments in America.

After Chapel Hill, Fleming married and started a family that would grow to four children. He secured a teaching job at Miami University in Ohio. South Carolina beckoned. In the 1970s, Fleming returned home to serve as headmaster of the Archibald Rutledge Academy in McClellanville. Always restless, Fleming now desired to launch a publication. The South, in the post-civil rights era, looked to be a dead cause. The New South, dramatized by the shining glass towers of Atlanta and its money-making *ethos*, represented the future. Robert E. Lee and the 10th amendment, William Faulkner's black dirt Mississippi or Flannery O'Connor's red clay Georgia, were relics of a romanticized past as was the formidable literary legacy of the Fugitive-Agrarians.

Fleming and Wilson, along with the versatile M.E. Bradford, looked to rekindle a conservative Southern tradition in music, literature, theology, history—and even politics. Fleming, in fact, hoped the *Southern Partisan* would become the *New Yorker* of the region. Tom and Clyde published two issues in 1979 before bowing to financial reality. Fleming had to sell his share to Richard Quinn, a noted political consultant and colleague of Lee Atwater. *Southern Partisan* would continue to be published for some years as an attractive, glossy magazine in full color. The publication was bolstered significantly by mostly anonymous contributions by Thomas Landess and by Bradford. But *Southern Partisan* became a pro-Republican Party publication, an institution that Fleming and Wilson never cared for.

Fleming, in 1984, moved his family to Rockford, Illinois, becoming managing editor at *Chronicles,* a monthly magazine published by the Rockford Institute, a pro-family think tank. It was founded in 1977 by Leopold Tyrmand, a Polish-born novelist. Publications such as *The New York Review of Books* decided what books are worth reviewing and as such, which volumes grabbed the attention of a distracted mass media and their reading public. *Chronicles* originally started out as a monthly devoted to book reviews. It could help break the monopoly the New York crowd had on that industry. A tall order.

Tyrmand died in 1985 of a heart attack. He was 64. Fleming was appointed editor. He revamped *Chronicles*. It would now be a monthly journal of opinion along the lines of *Commentary* and *American Spectator*. The Chapel Hill gang—Wilson, Kopff, Reed, and Sam Francis were all on board. Tom and Sam were brothers-in-arms. Sam shared Fleming's and Wilson's dislike of the GOP. He was also a political animal. Democracy was the hand that's been dealt to you. One has no choice but to play it.

While in Rockford, Fleming made another significant ally. Paul Gottfried, a political scientist, was now teaching at Rockford College. A native of Bridgeport, Connecticut and a graduate of both Yale and Yeshiva University, Gottfried started out as a student of Central European thought, writing a book on the German political scientist Carl Schmitt and later a study of Hegel's influence on American conservatism. Gottfried did not start out as a right winger. In the early Seventies he was a fan of neoconservatism, especially as articulated on the pages of *Commentary*. Paul was also a Reaganite. In 1980, he served as an alternate delegate for Ronald Reagan in the Illinois contingent at that year's Republican National Convention.

In 1988, Gottfried and Fleming collaborated on a monograph, *The Conservative Movement,* for Twayne Publishers. That volume detailed a mostly optimistic history of the movement, but one also critical of a triumphant neoconservatism. In the 1980s, conservatives seemed united. Late in the decade, cracks appeared. Prominent was the role of American foreign policy in the coming post-Cold War era. Most establishment conservatives would support a "democracy promotion" policy, while the paleos attempted to revive the pre-World War II America First. That wasn't all. Gottfried and Fleming maintained that deep cultural divisions existed between the neocons and the earlier Barry Goldwater movement.

The neocons were in New York City and Washington. The paleos preferred the South and the rural Midwest. The neocons were moved by democratic capitalism and a "nation of immigrants" ideology. The paleos, Fleming and Gottfried wrote, were inspired by "the historical saga of flesh-and-blood men and women building a community on the frontier." Or as Clyde Wilson later maintained, the U.S. Constitution is only as good as the character of the people living under it.

Gottfried became part of Fleming's stable of writers. He, too, became friends with Sam Francis. During the Reagan years, Gottfried relocated to the Washington, D.C. area, where he held down a high-profile job as editor of *The World and I*, a thick glossy magazine supplement to the *Washington Times*. Francis, along with Bradford and Russell Kirk, were regular contributors. Gottfried, in time, became a severe critic of neoconservatism. That mattered. Norman Podhoretz, editor of *Commentary*, opposed Gottfried's potential appointment as a graduate school professor at George Washington University, claiming that the latter was not sufficiently supportive of Israel. The smear campaign worked. Gottfried, the father of five, was denied the post. He also fell short in a 1987 bid to become chairman of the National Endowment for the Humanities (NEH), a plum job that went instead to neoconservative Lynne Cheney, wife of a future vice president.

Gottfried retreated to a position at Elizabethtown College in Pennsylvania, where he maintained a prolific publishing career, including an expanded 1993 edition of *The Conservative Movement*, a volume even more critical of the neoconservative worldview and of their ability to corner monies dished out by well-endowed foundations. The revised edition received high praise from Richard Nixon, Pat Buchanan, and Murray Rothbard.

Gottfried, Wilson, Fleming, Chilton Williamson Jr., and Sam Francis rounded out a "Big Five" that represented the driving force behind the unlikely rise of paleoconservatism. There were other influences: Russell Kirk, Murray Rothbard, and M.E. Bradford, and, most important, Patrick Buchanan with his syndicated column and nightly appearances on *Crossfire*. His 1992 and 1996 presidential campaigns put the agenda, if not the tongue-twisting name, in the national spotlight.

In his 2008 memoir *Encounters*, Paul fondly remembered his longtime colleague. He wrote a chapter on his friendship with Sam, Russell Kirk, and Murray Rothbard, citing them for "their willingness to forego worldly success for what they believed as the truth." *Encounters* contained tributes to such giants as Kirk and Rothbard, plus Bradford, Robert Nisbet, Pat Buchanan, Eugene Genovese, Thomas Molnar, John Lukacs, and improbably enough, both Richard Nixon and Herbert Marcuse. In this book full of moving portraits of conservatism's fallen warriors, Gottfried's praise of Sam Francis stands out:

> At his best, Sam was a brilliant stylist and courageous analyst. Although my junior by five years, he was the contemporary on the American Right who shaped my thinking most decisively. As a frequent dinner guest at our home in Bethesda, Maryland, during my years of service at *The World and I*, and as someone who produced many provocative texts, Sam occupies a special place among my mentors. Whatever my personal setbacks, I resent what happened to him more than I do my own tribulations. While I have managed to survive my enemies, this was not true for my reclusive friend, who expressed unseasonable thoughts all too loudly.

3.

High Hopes

IN THE MID-1970S the Chapel Hill gang went their separate ways. Fleming, Wilson, and Kopff were young men starting their academic careers. Sam Francis would end up in journalism. Their paths would converge at *Chronicles*. These young scholars held out hope that American conservatism—stalled by Watergate—might yet slay the liberal beast and return the nation to its constitutional roots.

It was a challenging time to be a conservative. Richard Nixon, unlike Goldwater and Reagan, was leery of the right. (He believed that the Buckleyites were more dangerous than the John Birch Society members, as the former were more articulate and not prone to conspiracy theories.) Still, Nixon's Silent Majority raised hopes that Middle American armies might yet recapture their nation from the East Coast elites. Weeds were beginning to sprout from the concrete jungle of Washington. This wall-to-wall leftist city would see the birth of conservative-leaning think tanks. The American Enterprise Institute traced its origins to the late 1930s, before taking off in the early 1970s under the leadership of William Baroody, Sr. In 1973 came the Heritage Foundation. Both were designed to counter the left in the battle of ideas and score political victories.

In 1977, Sam Francis, still two years away from his doctorate, joined Heritage as a junior fellow. Years later, when Sam emerged as the spokesman for right wing populism, his friends would kid him about working for the D.C. establishment. That wasn't the case in the Seventies when Heritage was an outsider think tank.

With the job, Sam had his foot in the door. He was a respectable conservative. Heritage was initially bankrolled by Joseph Coors, the Colorado-based beer baron, for a modest sum of $250,000. From the beginning, it was in the mainstream of establishment conservative thought, dedicated to "free enterprise, limited government, individual freedom, traditional American values, and a strong national defense."

With conservative discontent at a peak during the Nixon-Ford-Carter years, the times were ripe for a right-of-center think tank. Heritage took off under the energetic leadership of Edwin Feulner, a Chicago native who proved to be an accomplished fundraiser. Feulner traveled the globe, including anti-communist Taiwan and South Korea, securing hefty funds for the Heritage upstarts. By 1980, its budget exceeded $5.3 million. As of this writing, that number stands at $87 million. It's a profitable place to work.

Like *National Review*, Heritage sought to define American conservatism. It stood for tax cuts, "smart" immigrants, and plenty of recommendations of where to cut the fat from the budget. As the new Cold War of the Eighties heated up, Heritage was well-positioned. The U.S. should not just contain Soviet expansionism, it should work to beat back the Soviet Empire on all corners of the globe, including Eastern Europe. Heritage articulated a thorough de-regulation of much of the American economy. It championed privatization of Social Security and other entitlement programs. To deal with America's failing public schools, Heritage proposed school choice and vouchers for low-income students to attend private schools, plus tax credits and enterprise zones to revitalize crime-ridden inner-city neighborhoods such as New York City's South Bronx.

When Reagan was elected president in 1980, Heritage eagerly provided a blueprint for fulfilling the Gipper's mandate. In late 1981, the think tank proudly proclaimed that 66 percent of its recommendations had been adopted by the administration. Reagan confidant Edwin Meese was a fan and conservatives took to wearing Adam Smith neckties to dramatize their fidelity to free enterprise.

Was Sam Francis at home at Heritage? A strong anti-communist, Sam certainly supported the rollback of the Soviet Empire. His views, in time, were far more sledgehammer in nature than Heritage's mere policy prescriptions. Sam became a protectionist on trade, a restrictionist on immigration, and America First in foreign policy. He was a former Cold War hawk opposing wars in Iraq, Somalia, the former Yugoslavia, Afghanistan, and Iraq yet again. He held little hope for vouchers and school choice. Rollback, to Sam, meant the end to busing orders which greatly riled American society in the late 1960s and early '70s. That position was considered right wing, a place Heritage has never wanted to be.

Working at Heritage, Sam lived the bachelor's life in the humming Washington, D.C. area. The man was a dutiful foot soldier. He wrote papers critical of the Carter administration's plans to ease inflation. He studied the Soviet Union's "strategy of terror" which later became a long essay published in a book form. In Washington, Sam made new friends including Louis March, then working as a staffer on Capitol Hill. The two friends were later joined by Jerry Woodruff, a journalist who edited *Middle American News*, a monthly publication featuring hard-hitting columnists from the right, with Sam as the featured author.

It was a heady time. Jimmy Carter had been elected president; the Democrats controlled both houses of Congress. Conservatives like being in the opposition. Sam and his colleagues were determined to make the most of it—and to have plenty of fun along the way. March's tribute to Sam, given at a memorial service in 2005, captures those carefree days:

> Twenty-eight years ago, a colleague had complimentary tickets to one of those conservative appreciation dinners in Washington. As a young Senate staffer, I jumped at the chance to go. Jimmy Carter had been sworn in as president, and we movement

conservatives were digging in to promote our principles in the face of a White House and Congress dominated by the left.

I remember those good old days—we were the hardcore conservatives, the early-day paleocons. Our situation back then brings to mind Shakespeare's words, *"We few, we happy few, we band of brothers."* Leaving the dinner, my colleague spotted an old buddy from the North Carolina Conservative Society and hailed him over. He was Sam Francis. Afterwards my colleague remarked that Sam was a mere shadow of his former self— "He must have lost about a hundred pounds!" Sam was actually slender.

Sam Francis and his friends were outsiders. These young men began forming doubts over the effectiveness of any conservative movement:

This was 1977. About a week later, Sam called and invited me to lunch. We hit it off and then some. We'd read the same books and had similar interests. Fellow Southerners, we both had forebears who suffered the late unpleasantness a scant hundred years before—so there were no illusions about big government beneficence! We had both been in Washington a matter of weeks. As time passed, we found ourselves meeting for lunch two or more times a week, sometimes in the Senate cafeteria, sometimes at a Capitol Hill watering hole called The Man in the Green Hat. Patrons were packed like sardines, so Sam and I began taking walks around the block after lunch, swapping stories and expounding on our politically incorrect ideas.

It was on those walks, in the 1970s, that we tumbled to the realization that the Washington "leadership" of the conservative movement was woefully out of sync with its grassroots supporters in the heartland. We wondered why. Sometimes we would talk ourselves around the block two or three times until one of us would say, "Don't we have jobs somewhere?" Then he would walk one way, back to the Heritage Foundation, and I in the other direction, to that bloated bastion of imperial democracy, the United States Senate.

March's memories are all good ones. Sam was a friend, a wit; he was generous with his modest funds:

> Sam was at his best during the regular beer bashes I used to throw at my bachelor pad. As they wound down, after midnight, the ten or fifteen lingering diehards would gather round and Sam would hold forth, dropping droll Francis witticisms left and right. Yet, however unsparing his banter in those days, it was not unkind—he had such a way with words. Usually the conversation continued into the very wee hours, and we'd go out to breakfast at Bob and Edith's or that old truck stop-type restaurant on Route 1 near Crystal City—which, sadly, is now an Afghan restaurant.
>
> One day at our usual after-work haunt, I was a bit down in the mouth. I'd been invited out to California and needed an extra $500 that I didn't have to make the trip. I had never been to California. Sam spoke up: "I'll lend you the money. I have the $500, you need it, end of story." I was amazed. And if you knew what a fastidiously frugal fellow he was, you'd be too! But that is how I got to California the first time—courtesy of Sam. Though he was my *de facto* banker,

he would accept no perks beyond repayment. In fact, he allowed me to spring for lunch only once—to celebrate his newly conferred Ph.D.

Above all, there was the man's serious side. Sam knew where he stood. He was a man of the West, with no ambiguities:

> Then we discovered Jerry Woodruff. Sam, Jerry, and I were like three peas in a pod—we'd pile in the car and head out to a party, movie, used bookstore, or some bargain-basement eatery. Ladies would be present on occasion, necessitating two or even three cars between us. Of course, back then we weren't paying the price of empire at the gas pumps. From time to time, we would visit a firing range. A good Southerner, Sam was at ease with arms. He was a very good shot. I asked how he became so. He replied, "When you aim, think of the enemies of our civilization."

There was unity on most fronts. Conservatives and Republicans alike mocked the Carter Administration. The right was pro-life and in favor of prayer in school. Anti-communism remained paramount. Rollback of the Soviet Empire, especially in the nine Christian nations behind the Iron Curtain, superseded all, including the social issues. Buckley, still reeling from Goldwater's landslide defeat in 1964, welcomed neoconservatives into the fold. These were New York Trotskyites who had moved over to become Cold War liberals. In time the AEI, Heritage Foundation, and *National Review* all fell, in the eyes of bitter paleoconservatives, under neoconservative domination.

Named so by the leftist sociologist Michael Harrington, neoconservatives were refugees from the Great Society left. By the late Sixties, such liberals, represented by Irving Kristol at *The Public Interest* and Norman Podhoretz at *Commentary*, were disgusted by the rise of the New Left and its criticism of Israel's victory in the 1967 war and the ensuing occupation of former Egyptian and Syrian territory. They opposed affirmative action. There was the crime wave in large cities and the hooligan-like behavior by middle-class students on such prestigious campuses as Columbia University, long home base for Lionel Trilling, a legendary English professor and neoconservative favorite.

Neoconservatives boasted an impressive array of celebrity scholars: Gertrude Himmelfarb, Kristol's wife and a prominent historian; Jeanne J. Kirkpatrick; crime expert James Q. Wilson; sociologist Peter Berger; the Rev. John Richard Neuhaus; and Harvey Mansfield, a political scientist who held down the fort at Harvard University. Kirkpatrick's 1979 *Commentary* essay, "Dictatorships and Double Standards," a withering critique of President Carter's human-rights based foreign policy, caught the eye of then-candidate Ronald Reagan. In 1981, the latter, a keen political thinker who poured through such conservative journals of opinion as *National Review, American Spectator,* and *Human Events,* appointed Kirkpatrick as his high-profile American ambassador to the United Nations.

Neoconservatives hit the ground running. Such stalwarts as Russell Kirk and Pat Buchanan at first welcomed them as a force for good, especially considering their location in wall-to-wall liberal New York City. An early dissent came from James Burnham, still serving as senior editor at *National Review.* The neoconservatives, he cautioned, still displayed "the gestalt of liberalism," clinging, as Sam later termed it, "to its emotional, psychic and moral reflexes." Conservative, yes, but also wary of any right-wing populism brewing in the Heartland.

A major debate of that decade was between Harry Jaffa and M.E. Bradford over the single word that has forever tormented the American experience: *Equality*. Both were academics, Jaffa at Claremont McKenna College in California, Bradford at the University of Dallas. Jaffa was a Goldwaterite. He is credited with penning the man's legendary 1964 acceptance speech at the Republican Party National Convention in San Francisco, where

Goldwater lashed out at his opponents, proclaiming defiantly: "Let me remind you that extremism in the defense of liberty is no vice." Goldwater never had a chance of winning the presidency, and this broadside was no help.

Bradford was heir to a Texas family that had been in the Lone Star State for five generations. While a graduate student at Vanderbilt University, Bradford happily signed on to the Agrarian conservatism of his beloved mentor, Donald Davidson. Bradford was an English professor, a scholar on Allen Tate, Caroline Gordon, Andrew Lytle, and the short fiction of William Faulkner. An authentic genius, Bradford also ventured deeply into American history, becoming a preeminent scholar of the Founding Era, especially in his 1982 book, *A Worthy Company*, which included scholarly biographies of the 55 men who signed the U.S. Constitution. Bradford discovered that the Founders, whether from New York and New Hampshire or South Carolina and Georgia, all dreaded a centralized regime snuffing out local cultures and their ways.

Equality. What does the word mean? To what extent should the federal government pursue it as a goal? Is it even possible at all? In the debate Bradford's position collided with the legacy of both Abraham Lincoln and the Warren Court. Jaffa was wary of a literalist reading of the Constitution championed by Robert Bork and Antonin Scalia and earlier by Bradford, Willmoore Kendall, Russell Kirk, and Frank Meyer. Jaffa maintained that the Declaration and the U.S. Constitution were inseparable. According to an online biographer, Jaffa "[believed] that the Declaration of Independence and the Constitution share a relationship whereby the latter is intended to preserve the principles of the former." Hence, the Declaration should figure into Supreme Court decisions. Bradford rejected such thinking. The justices should adhere only to the Constitution's original intent. During the 1980s Bradford traveled the nation, giving a series of lectures later collected in a book of that same name: *Original Intentions: On the Making and Ratification of the U.S. Constitution*. Equality under the law is all any society can hope to achieve.

Bradford was a scholar. However, his family members had wanted him to become involved in Texas politics. In both 1968 and 1972, Bradford supported the George Wallace candidacies. In the early Seventies, he was, believe it or not, chairman of the Dallas County Democratic Party. By 1976 Bradford had joined the Republican Party. That year he supported Ronald Reagan's maverick candidacy against President Gerald Ford. Reagan lost the nomination. He won the Texas primary by a landslide margin, carrying every one of the Lone Star's 254 counties. In 1980, Reagan was nominated and elected. Bradford's work for Reagan in both campaigns didn't go unnoticed. He was the early favorite to be nominated as chairman for the National Endowment for the Humanities (NEH). Bradford had the support of Senators Jesse Helms, John P. East, Dan Quayle, and Orin Hatch, and William F. Buckley, Jr. Bradford was a contributor to *National Review* and Buckley was on good terms with Southern conservatives.

Neoconservatives, however, opposed Bradford. They had their own candidate, William J. Bennett, then a Democrat and director of The National Humanities Center, a private research institution in North Carolina. Bennett would swing federal largess, grant monies, their way. With the help of A.M. Rosenthal, editor of the *New York Times,* and George F. Will, columnist for the *Washington Post,* the neoconservatives launched an intense anti-Bradford campaign. It focused on the man's past support for Wallace and especially his essays critical of the Lincoln legacy. Buckley, too, was now in opposition, as was Edwin Feulner. The campaign reached all the way to a weekday CBS News segment, anchored by a disbelieving Jessica Savitch.

Neocon apparatchiks destroyed Bradford's nomination files several times. The Reaganites got cold feet. They assumed that with the neocons they were getting valuable intellectuals to their side such as the Democrats had always had. The GOP was too philistine for Bradford. The California car dealer who managed Reagan's appointment paperwork thought that Bradford's article on Edmund

Spenser's "The Fairie Queen" was about homosexuals. Bradford withdrew, resuming his extensive teaching, writing, and lecturing duties. The conservative wars raging to this day were on.

During the Seventies, Sam Francis remained an unknown. In the equality debate he sided with Bradford over Jaffa and was front and center in defending Bradford for the NEH post. Decades later, Tom Fleming recalled that bitter struggle:

> As an assistant to Senator John East, Sam worked tirelessly, both on the Hill and among conservatives, to support Bradford's nomination, but to no avail. Too many true-blue "Reagan" conservatives either did not care or simply looked the other way. This was the first of many defeats in which Sam showed himself an American Cato.

Sam was not sentimental, but he truly looked up to Bradford. When the latter died an untimely death in 1993 at age 58, Francis, now a syndicated columnist, wrote eloquently about his fellow conservative:

> In the states and in the souls where Confederate flags still fly, they fluttered at half-mast for M.E. Bradford, gentleman, scholar, political thinker and Good Old Rebel. The legacy he left to an America now being reconstructed to suit political correctness and political expediency is one that not only his Southern friends, students, colleagues and admirers should receive. The two countries he loved so much—America and the South—need to take their stand on ground he so unflinchingly defended.

It was Bradford's intimate knowledge of Sam's homeland that deeply moved the columnist:

> Mel Bradford's South had the hard beauty of old women who have buried their sons, of Texas frontiersmen who have fought Comanches, of small farmers who worked barren fields and died at Shiloh for a cause that could not win. His was the South that sings the human tragedy, a drama that never leaves the stage no matter how rich, powerful, and progressive its actors and spectators might swell.

In Bradford's presence, the old America, every square inch, came alive:

> To talk with Mel was to make an odyssey in time. He would ask a young man whom he had never met the Southerner's traditional first question—"Where are you from?"—and then proceed to tell him about whatever place that was: its history, its geography, what kind of crops its soil supported, what sort of people settled it, what its politics were in the War Between the States and why—and he could speak almost as much about New England or the Midwest. He knew the South and America by county and creek, and in debate with him the easy generalizations and abstractions in which our history is usually couched crumbled before his knowledge.

There was bitterness over Bradford's before-mentioned failure to chair the NEH and the corresponding rise of neoconservatives, who placed an emphasis, in Sam's words, on "propositions," "social contracts," and "higher laws." To Bradford and Francis, America was something entirely different. "A society, [Bradford argued] is 'grown, not made,' undesigned by human reason, 'bound by blood, place and history' and should be governed in accord with them and their norms," Sam wrote.

That philosophy collided headfirst into the realities of 20th century America, an immigrant nation constructed around democracy and equality. Francis readily acknowledged that Bradford's world of family and soil faced a long, difficult road ahead:

> Mel Bradford was a traditionalist whose teaching leaves us a gentler inheritance. It may be long before Americans and their leaders have the wisdom and the grace to take it up, but when we do the banners this Good Old Rebel will unfurl once again.

Bradford echoed Richard Weaver's description of the American South as being built around social bond individualism. The Southern joining of both community and individualism was something unique and healthy and should be encouraged. Artistic expression must take place within the framework of the larger community with those agreed-upon intangibles: culture, language, history, music, literature, folk tales, manners, morals, and a way of life.

Bradford was a literary critic. Power was Sam's central theme. To Sam, equality was a blunt instrument for power. Equality, in American terms, means equality of results, which translate into a nation in constant conflict. Weaver quoted a saying common in the old Virginia: If all men are created equal was ever taken at face value, it would blow up the entire planet. Only it didn't. Outside of the Western orbit, nations and cultures are not centered around notions of equality. Distinctions of rank, hierarchy, class, religion, ethnicity, race, and gender matter. The world hasn't exploded. At home, however, meet America, summer of 1964 onward.

Sam found flaws with the right's critique of equality. Such intellectuals as Thomas Fleming and Stephen Goldberg focused on the sociobiological and anthropological aspects of the issue. Is equality of results possible? Are men equal? That was not the point. Equality is a winning card for liberals. It is a political weapon, designed to tear down old pieties and create new and even newer constituencies, voting blocs that keep liberals both in power and able to expand power.

Francis was a modernist; he accepted the urban-industrial order. However, Sam's America was the turn-of-the-century world of shopkeepers, small business owners, farmers, and professionals all living under the family unit as a husband-wife-children arrangement. Everything flowed from there. To make a revolution, the old order had to be obliterated. As with old-fashioned conservatives, the Enlightenment, to Sam, was not a source of liberation, but instead an engine of destruction:

> In the Enlightenment and in much of classical liberalism, the target was the state—the established churches, aristocracies, guilds, and dynasties of the eighteenth century. When liberation from these political "chains" failed to bring about the promised land, the target became the economy—private property, classical economics, and the distribution of wealth—and it was mainly an economic target that the Progressives had in their sights. In the twentieth century, the target shifted yet again to social and cultural environment—the family, the school, religion, social class, and race as a social phenomenon. Eventually, we can predict egalitarians will discover that nature itself is the source of inequality. Whether egalitarians, recognizing at last that inequality is ultimately rooted in man's nature, accept that lesson, or whether, through genetic engineering and state-funded lobotomies, they launch yet another revolt against inequality and against nature itself will depend less on who and how many really believe in the egalitarian lie than on who stands to gain from wielding the egalitarian sword.

Francis's essay "Equality as a Political Weapon" was published in 1989. Establishment Conservatives had other things on their minds. Paramount was prevailing over the Soviet Union. The Bradford-Jaffa debate was quickly forgotten in the euphoria of

1980 when the nerdy losers of American life—conservatives—became winners. Liberals never liked Jimmy Carter, a South Georgia peanut farmer, for intruding on their Democratic Party. The Left preferred Ted Kennedy as the 1980 nominee. Even worse was Ronald Reagan, long dismissed as a B-grade movie actor known for "Bedtime for Bonzo," and a right-wing warmonger from right-wing Southern California.

The nerdy losers saw their candidate upend a sitting president in a 44-state landslide, while the long somnolent GOP gained control of the U.S. Senate. For years, William F. Buckley, Jr., Reagan's longtime friend, referred to that election as "the glorious fourth," signifying its November 4th date. Conservative unity had been achieved. Anti-communism was the glue holding that fractious movement together and in the young Sam Francis, the right had an energetic foot soldier.

One of the surprise victories of 1980 belonged to John P. East, an obscure college professor at East Carolina University in Greenville, North Carolina, who scored an upset win, defeating the incumbent Democrat Robert Morgan to become the Tar Heel state's junior Senator. East, a native of Springfield, Illinois, took a circular route to the Senate. He received a Bachelor of Arts from Earlham College in Indiana. After graduating in 1953, he married and was commissioned as an officer in the United States Marines Corp. At Camp Lejeune, tragedy struck. The young officer was stricken with polio, which left him wheelchair-bound for the rest of his life. East carried on. He received a law degree from the Illinois College of Law, before earning an M.A. and Ph.D. in political science from the University of Florida. In 1964, he settled down as an academic. In Greenville, East fell into the GOP's circle, running an unsuccessful 1966 campaign for the U.S. House of Representatives.

Like Sam, East was a dedicated rightist. Over the years, the professor had published essays on Russell Kirk, Richard Weaver, Frank Meyer, Willmoore Kendall, Leo Strauss, Eric Voegelin and Ludwig von Mises, all collected in a 1986 volume, *The American Conservative Movement: The Philosophical Founders*. East was right-wing, someone who, if possible, would overthrow the entire post-1932 liberal regime. Tom Ellis, director of the Raleigh-based Congressional Club, an astute political operative who engineered Reagan's 1976 upset win over Gerald Ford in that state's first-ever GOP presidential primary, tapped East to be Morgan's challenger. Ellis believed that Republican candidates should come from the Democrats' eastern heartland. Cut into the Dems lead there and pile up big numbers in the GOP-leaning western counties.

The 1980 election was light years removed from today's world: no cable TV, talk radio, or social media. Advertising was done through newspaper ads. Polls were a rarity. On the eve of the election, one poll had Morgan with a double-digit lead, another had the race even. The latter turned out to be correct. East was elected by a razor-thin 11,000-vote margin, scoring 49.96 percent to Morgan's 49.38 percent.

The race itself was punishing. This was the first year that the religious right, in the form of the Moral Majority, dove headfirst into elective politics. It was considered common courtesy that if a state had two senators from different parties, the senator not facing re-election would sit out the campaign. Helms did not campaign for East. As an avatar for the nascent Moral Majority, Helms sent out a letter via a mass mailing hailing East as a "good Christian." After the election, the defeated incumbent ran into Helms on Capitol Hill. "Well, if it isn't that good Christian, Jesse Helms," Morgan bitterly cried out.

That slim victory proved pivotal to Sam's budding career. With East's victory, Francis's professional life would take a sharp turn. The Heritage Foundation provided a farm system of young analysts ready to graduate to Capitol Hill as congressional aides. East needed a staffer who was a speechwriter, a foreign policy expert, and a fellow right winger. On all counts, Sam fit the bill. Goodbye to the solitude of the think tank. Hello to the switchblade world of Washington, D.C. politics. Neither John P. East nor Sam Francis would duck the challenge.

4.

Burnhamite

IN THE 1980S SAM FRANCIS'S career as a writer took off. Ensconced in Senator East's office, he was a top aide to a rookie senator whose articulate conservatism gained him media coverage. Pundits nicknamed East "Helms on Wheels" or called Helms "North Carolina's liberal senator."

Sam's friends also moved in creative directions. Reed at Chapel Hill began publishing a series of essay collections explaining to curious outsiders that the South—New or Old—remained distinctly Southern in its folkways, religion, and politics. In an exchange of letters, Reed took his friend Francis to task for promoting non-democratic leanings. Sam cheerfully responded that Reed was correct: The columnist did *not* believe in democracy as an ideal form of government, preferring instead the examples of 5th century B.C. Athens and the Roman Republic of Cincinnatus. It was all done with good humour. *Southern Partisan* carried on after Fleming's departure, aided by contributions by Bradford and Landess, under the editorship of Oran P. Smith and Chris Sullivan.

With Reagan's landslide win, conservatism, long dismissed as old lady in sneakers, was now "in." "What is *theese* conservatism?," William Rusher recalled an Italian journalist asking him as the 1980 results poured in. The rise of the right allowed Francis to become a contributor to two notable books: *The New Right Papers* and *Why the South Will Survive*. Robert Whitaker, a South Carolina author and political activist, solicited essays for a collection, *The New Right Papers*. Published by St. Martin's, a leading Manhattan house, the book was an eclectic collection that included such longtime *National Review* hands as Rusher and Jeffrey Hart, plus voices of an emerging paleoconservatism: Fleming, Wilson, and Sam Francis.

In 1980, surviving contributors to the 1930 Agrarian manifesto *I'll Take My Stand* were invited to a 50th anniversary celebration at Vanderbilt University. Lyle Lanier, Andrew Lytle, and Robert Penn Warren attended, accompanied by Cleanth Brooks, literary critic and Warren's co-editor of the *Southern Review*. The reunion was poignant. It received national attention, including a handsome spread in *Time* magazine. Warren, who in 1985 would be appointed America's first Poet Laureate, had no desire to defend the old cause. However, Lytle, once "the kid" of the Agrarian fraternity, still subscribed to a Jeffersonian society built around small landowners as superior in all ways— economic, communal, cultural, and spiritual— to the long-ago triumph of an urban-industrial order.

The *I'll Take My Stand* anniversary proved the impetus for Clyde Wilson's edited collection, *Why the South Will Survive*. Wilson secured essays from Lytle, Bradford, Fleming, Reed, Francis, the prolific Flannery O'Connor scholar Marion Montgomery, Cleanth Brooks, George Garrett, and Fred Hobson, a liberal champion of the New South. With the two publications, Sam hit the ground running. His literate, hard-hitting and energetic prose style was already formed, setting the stage for 25 years of arresting commentary and insight.

Sam was asked to give a foreign policy essay to the Wilson collection. With the 1979 Soviet invasion of Afghanistan and that year's seizing of American hostages by Iran's new Islamic regime, the détente of the 1970s had been shattered. The shipyard strikes by Poland's Solidarity labor union focused the world's attention on Eastern Europe. The "new Cold War" was confirmed by the incredible events of 1983: the deployment of American cruise missiles in Western Europe to counter the presence of Soviet SS-20 missiles in Eastern Europe, the Soviet downing of a South Korean civilian airliner over the Sea of Japan, the U.S. invasion of Grenada designed to overthrow a Marxist-Leninist regime in that tiny Caribbean country. Plus the breakdown of U.S.—U.S.S.R. arms reduction talks that brought East-West tensions to their most serious levels since the 1962 Cuban Missile crisis.

Sam's assignment was to illustrate how the conservative Southern tradition might be an influence for a healthy American foreign policy. He acknowledged the awkwardness of the task: The Southern-born presidents of the 20th century— Woodrow Wilson, Lyndon Johnson, and Jimmy Carter— had been embarrassments. According to Sam, they were foolishly utopian. Wilson had his dreams of global democracy, all to be brought about by America's participation in the "war to ends all wars," plus American membership in the League of Nations, a body that critics claimed would have the United States fighting alongside Great Britain in the latter's imperial struggles throughout the world. Carter placed an unrealistic emphasis on human rights, one that resulted in American allies in Iran and Nicaragua being overthrown and replaced with shrill anti-American regimes. Then there was Lyndon B. Johnson, who plunged America headfirst into Vietnam in yet another bid to fight Communism and extend democracy.

Francis counseled a return to America First. The United States need not use its power to advance democracy or human rights. Instead, it should only secure the safety of its own people and institutions. Where did America go wrong? Sam cited the triumph of the "Puritan Yankee establishment," entrenched at the Department of State. Their millenarian worldview sought to remake the planet in America's image. Which meant one war after another. And if not a military war then an economic sanctions war against nations that violate human rights. That policy, Francis admitted, had successful monetary results for some:

> In the twentieth century, the millenarian authors have four times persuaded a reluctant populace that it should go to war, not for its own interest, but for the interests of Europe, Korea, and Vietnam. The lofty

rhetoric of internationalism, world peace and human rights has been matched by ruthless bargaining for economic, political, and military power.

Being a war merchant is a lucrative business. Vietnam, however, is where the Puritan establishment lost its nerve. They went to war, but without fighting to win:

> If the war were really a struggle against aggression, then why not a permanent end to the aggressors' ability to make war? Avoiding this unthinkable implication, the authors of our Vietnam policy insisted on defending their course on the grounds that the war was a struggle for democracy, for progress in the Third World, for the millenarian vision.

What could the benighted Southland offer? The South was able to teach lessons to a nation unschooled in tragedy. If America represented success upon success, the American South "was unique in having experienced military defeat, foreign occupation, and the suppression of its institutions." The region's tragic past is far more representative of the world's condition than America's longtime belief in happy endings. Belief in original sin matters.

Such pessimistic realism, Sam added, "tends to distrust power and the ability of statesmen to reorder the world because it ultimately distrusts man himself." Belief in God, yes; in man, never. Belief in public order matters, too. William Faulkner loved to confirm that in his native Mississippi, the past isn't dead, it isn't even past. That means a people with something more to defend than democracy or freedom:

> A social unit does not exist through its physical borders or the sum of its individual residents. Its existence is historical, reaching into the past as well as the future, and any calculation of its particular interests must not omit those of a historical nature.

> In foreign affairs it is not enough to establish the present material interest of a particular sector. The primary concern in foreign policy must be in the protection of the historic character and identity of the community.

Is that possible in 21st century America?

> The lesson is what the South, and only the South, can teach America, has in a sense always tried teaching it and has never been able to teach it. The failure of the South in this respect is at least as significant as the other, bloodier, and more dramatic failure that has haunted and informed the region for the past century or more.

The essay dramatized Sam's persistent pessimism. Did Francis believe this new, two-party South viewed foreign policy any differently from the rest of the nation? During the 1980s, Southern Democrats, along with the GOP minority, remained anti-communist, supporting the Reagan Doctrine of giving arms to anti-communist guerillas in Central America, Asia, and southern Africa. When the Cold War ended, the region did not sign up for America First. (Indeed, the South, in the late 1930s, was conspicuous for not joining the highly popular America First Committee of that era. They were ready to fight Germany.)

Beginning in the 1990s and especially after the September 11, 2001 terrorist attack, the South supported wars for democracy in both Afghanistan and Iraq. The new, one-party GOP South remained hawkish. Were Connecticut-born George H.W. Bush and George W. Bush ever true Southerners? Then there are the natives: Lindsey Graham's endless intervention on one end, Rand Paul's America First on the other.

For *The New Right Papers,* Sam was on more familiar ground: that of a cultural warrior, a spokesman for the beleaguered proletariat of fly-over country. "Message From MARS" was inspired by the research of Donald Warren, a University of Michigan sociologist who studied the voting habits of those white working-class troops who gave Nixon and Reagan their landslide victories and who also formed the backbone of the unsuccessful Goldwater and George Wallace candidacies.

Who were they? What did they fear? What did they want? MARS (Middle America Radicals) were disgusted by the nation's rapid descent into barbarism. Crime, inner city and college campus rioting, school busing orders, inflation, welfare payments, the humiliating defeat in Vietnam— MARS were overwhelmed by the social revolution upending a once-stable nation. The "Father Knows Best" family unit was being ridiculed in such documentaries as "The Louds" and such throw-away comedies as "Three's Company" and "Maud." The New Class celebrated a promiscuous lifestyle that mocked the pieties of the "poor, but proud" working-class Mom-Pop-children family unit. MARS, in fact, dreaded the future. They had become strangers in a strange land, a feeling of hopelessness replacing the old optimism. As Sam quoted Warren:

> MARS are a distinct group partly because of their view of government as favoring both the rich and the poor simultaneously. MARS are distinct in the depth of their feeling that the middle class has been seriously neglected. If there was one single summation of the MARS perspective, it is reflected in a statement which was read to respondents: The rich give in to the demands of the poor, and the middle-income people have to pay the bill.

In the late 1970s and early '80s, economic concerns were paramount: unemployment, inflation, interest rates— the middle-class dream was falling apart. "Message from MARS" reflects those anxieties. Immigration, the anti-Western culture war, and demographic upheaval were not yet in the forefront. Sam's strategy also reflected the ethos of the bourgeois America he supported:

> The strategic objective of the New Right must be the localization, privatization, and decentralization of the managerial apparatus of power. This means a dismantling of the corporate, educational, labor and media bureaucracies; a devolution to more modest-scale organizational units; and a reorientation of federal rewards from mass-scale units to smaller and more local ones.

With the emphasis on privatization and decentralization, much of this sounds like a policy paper issued by the Heritage Foundation, but as always Sam was the culture warrior. Culture and economics went hand-in-hand. Towards that end, Sam called for a "domestic ethic [to] lay the basis for a more harmonious relationship between employer and worker, since the place of work itself can be portrayed as an institution no less central than the family or local community." Quoting Goethe, Sam ended the essay with a return to his now-favorite theme. Rule or be ruled. One must be the hammer or the anvil. Francis advised the MARS constituency to wield the big stick:

> A key element in the success of the New Right will be its ability to focus on how the establishment uses its apparatus of power in the media, corporations, and schools for political domination and exploitation. This has been made clear with regard to the bureaucracy and the unions, but other institutional supports of the liberal managerial elite need exposure as well.

Francis rejected both the free market ideology of the libertarians and the "stabilization" of the Democratic/Republican elite. His vision was a combination of *Wall Street Journal*-style economic growth and Main Street traditional morality. Francis also floated the idea of a strong presidency. His worldview was still being formed:

> In place of the hedonistic, pragmatist, relativist and secularized cosmopolitans of the present elite, the

> New Right should expound without compromise the ideas of institutions of the American ethos: hard work and self-sacrifice, morally based legislation and policies, and a public commitment to religious faith. In place of the faith in congressional supremacy, the New Right will favor a populist-based presidency able to cut through the present oligarchical establishment and to promote new intermediary institutions centered on Middle America.

The tone of both the Wilson and the Whitaker volumes was generally upbeat. Reagan's popularity did that to conservatives. Even Fleming, who soured on the GOP once his friend M.E. Bradford lost his bid to become the National Endowment of the Humanities (NEH) chairman, hoped that a conservative coalition of Midwesterners and Southerners might yet prevail. The title of the Wilson collection alone was defiant. Optimism is never characteristic of Southern literature. Still, Bradford would not spread despair:

> For the sake of memory, let us preserve the iconic things—buildings, monuments, gardens, rites, celebrations, and stories—which have defined us for over three hundred years as a people apart, and which carry the seeds of restoration. Objections to these reminders of an earlier South must be resisted at every turn and with every resource. The Romans taught their sons to look backward in order to prepare for the morrow. If our friends tell us that these days are dark, then we should recite something like the hopeful formula of Mr. [Donald] Davidson in his later years, one that he repeated to me many times over: that in order to get better, it must first get a good deal worse. With these priorities observed, our descendants may know that "we have not loosely, through silence, permitted things to pass away as in a dream."

Sam's career now took a decisive turn. He was published in books carrying a national circulation. A resumé that included a Ph.D. and a stint at the Heritage Foundation would take him places. Francis's rise was assisted by both publications, plus Fleming's unyielding loyalty, his status as a senior aide to a conservative favorite, having Gottfried as an editor of *The World & I*, and later by his coveted position as an editorial writer for the *Washington Times,* the must-read daily for conservatives in Washington. It was Sam's work, his development as a muscular and learned essayist, that made his fame inevitable.

Throughout the decade, Sam published steadily. In 1981 came his first monograph, *The Soviet Strategy of Terror*. In a brisk 78 pages, Sam declared that Soviet Communism and terrorism were natural allies. The Marxist-Leninist creed by nature is violent, calling for unending struggle and the overthrow of ruling elites. The Soviets, Sam acknowledged, were often hesitant over such violence. Moscow could not control the terrorists' organizations scattered across Europe, Asia, Africa, and Latin America. Moscow preferred political mobilization: nations needed to sign onto a socialist revolution headquartered in the Kremlin. Terrorism had its uses. "The purpose of terrorism is to terrorize," V.I. Lenin pronounced. Along with political revolution, street theater could weaken and bring down pro-Western regimes, all the way to Germany, Italy, and Japan.

During the 1970s, the West remained dependent on the Third World for raw materials to sustain its industrial base, including the military. Terrorist activity might destabilize the producing nations and give Moscow sway over their precious metals. Terrorist groups were too weak to help complete such a monumental task. Terrorism as employed by the Palestine Liberation Organization (PLO) at the 1972 Summer Olympics in Munich captured global headlines but could not shake Western resolve. Moscow remained half-hearted over terrorism. Punching an occasional police officer wasn't enough. By the early 1980s, however, the outcome was still in doubt.

Later in the decade, Sam made his first foray into the nation-breaking immigration issue. *Smuggling Revolution: The Sanctuary Movement in the United States* was another long essay studying the ongoing invasion. The essay did not focus on demographic change, its effect on the fading Nixon-Reagan coalition, or the anti-Western culture wars on college campuses. That came later. The pamphlet, published by the Capital Research Center, detailed how leftist legal organizations and liberal Protestants worked to bring illegal aliens into the United States, while seeking to prevent the government from deporting illegals already in the country. Their target was capitalist America and its inequities:

> Despite a tendency to appeal to Christian charity, common decency, and other moral and humanitarian motives in assisting illegal immigrants as "refugees," the Sanctuary movement operates within an elaborate ideological framework that connects it to political activism aimed at a radical transformation of American institutions and policies.

Read a quarter of a century later, the essay, although well-researched, is dated. Smuggling revolution? It came, it saw, it conquered. The United States may not be Marxist-Leninist. However, the Left's culture war is Marxist with a different twist, in that it is anti-Western, something the master would not approve. Since the 1980s, an immigrant voting bloc has helped to move American politics leftward, foot soldiers in the revolution. Ironically, the pamphlet was published in 1986, the same year that Congress addressed the illegal immigration issue. At the 1984 presidential debates, President Reagan floated an immigration deal that would grant amnesty to illegals in exchange for border security. Two years later a bipartisan bill was signed into law. Amnesty was granted, but the border remained wide open.

Earlier, in 1980, legislation introduced by Senator Edward Kennedy (D—MASS) allowed for huge increases in family reunification. An immigrant could come to America from an

Asian or Latin American nation and bring dozens of relatives—spouses, children, parents, grandparents, aunts, uncles, nephews, and cousins with him. Legal immigration skyrocketed, ushering in the triumph of multiculturalism. Neither the Reaganites nor congressional Republicans addressed legal immigration. Both parties continued to hail the U.S. as a nation of immigrants. The immigration issue would have to wait. And when it exploded, Sam Francis was front and center on the losing side.

The year 1984 saw Sam's second volume. Madison Books of Lanham, Maryland, brought out *Power and History: A Study of James Burnham*. Joe Sobran, a senior editor at *National Review* and a popular syndicated columnist, convinced the magazine's then Arts and Letters editor Chilton Williamson, Jr. to publish his review of Sam's book. The times were ripe for a Burnham biography. Détente was out. Anti-communism was in. With the Reagan Doctrine of funding anti-communist guerillas in Asia, Africa, and Latin America and with Eastern Europe restless, a key element of Burnham's thought had new life. Francis had now published the first biography of one of the twentieth century's most original and striking thinkers.

In the early Eighties, Burnham, who died in 1987, was in retirement. In 1978, he participated in the "Super Bowl Sunday" *Firing Line* debate between Ronald Reagan and William F. Buckley Jr. on Panama Canal treaty ratification. On the flight home from Columbia, South Carolina, where the debate took place, Burnham suffered a stroke. His writing career was over. In 1983, President Reagan awarded him the Presidential Medal of Freedom, declaring Burnham to be "one of the century's finest champions of freedom." Three years earlier, at *National Review's* triumphant 25th anniversary dinner, Buckley saluted Burnham as the principal intellectual influence on a publication that was now favorite reading of the President of the United States.

Burnham wasn't a household word, but his influence was enormous. His 1940 book, *The Managerial Revolution,* caught the attention of George Orwell, who later used the volume's theme—powerful nations would not be run by "the people," but instead by an entrenched managerial class of all things political, economic, and cultural—as inspiration for his legendary 1948 novel, *1984*. The son of a railroad executive, Burnham was a precocious scholar, graduating from Princeton University and Oxford and teaching at New York University all by age 28. He was also a young socialist, teaching T.S. Eliot and W.H. Auden by day and giving rip-roaring leftist speeches in his other life. Burnham was a stubborn thinker, a Trotskyite who once took on Trotsky himself in an exchange of angry letters.

By 1953, Burnham had given up on socialism. He took early retirement from NYU. A full-fledged anti-communist and the central prophet of a rollback policy, Burnham, by the late 1940s, worked for the Central Intelligence Agency (CIA), where he helped to formulate America's early Cold War policies. In the 1950s, Burnham also spoke out in defense of Senator Joseph McCarthy's Red-hunting crusade. That did it. Long a fixture on the New York intellectual scene as a contributor to *Partisan Review,* Burnham was declared *persona non grata* by Philip Rahv, the *PR* editor. Rahv spoke for the New York crowd when he pronounced that "James Burnham is finished."

Only he wasn't. In the mid-Fifties, the enterprising young Buckley, bored with his job at *The Freeman,* founded *National Review,* a publication designed to be a weekly conservative magazine of opinion, a counter to *The New Republic* and *The Nation.* Buckley, a youthful America Firster, was also a former CIA agent and a militant anti-communist, now ready to give up on his adolescent isolationism. Burnham became the young Buckley's main advisor. Burnham was a New York intellectual. As with other *NR* editors, he placed great hopes in the plain folk of the heartland. Burnham was convinced that the instinctive anti-communism of a freedom-loving people would provide the muscle to bring down the Soviet Empire.

Power and History received few reviews. As Sam's fame grew, the book was republished in 1999 by Claridge Press, a British firm, under the title*: James Burnham: Thinkers of Our Time*. The original title was better. Anti-communist yes, but *power* was key to Burnham's thought. That was the worldview that attracted Francis to Burnham's work. Power. Who has it? Who doesn't? Who gains power? Who keeps it? What is the fate of those without power? How do the powerless gain power? And *keep* power? And to what end?

The Managerial Revolution, to Burnham, came into being in the early decades of the twentieth century as the locus shifted from small businessmen and modest landowners to the managers of the urban-industrial order. The key year was 1932 and the election of Franklin D. Roosevelt. The New Deal solidified the triumph of the managerial state. The managers—those who controlled the economy, the bureaucracy, the corporate class, the entertainment, cultural and educational centers, the judiciary, and the military—held firmly to the levers of power. No election could change that.

The roots of the New Deal were in the Progressive Era, an elite revolution for centralization and expertise that took root following the Civil War. In Europe, that was achieved through the centralization of power by the unification of Italy and Germany. The massive movement of people from rural areas to industrial centers created an urban population boom. So, too, did European immigration into the United States. A bureaucracy—welfare payments, public schools, retirement benefits, unemployment checks—was necessary to control the masses. That's where the managers stepped in.

The Progressive Era saw the induction of the income tax and the direct election of United States senators. Woodrow Wilson's wartime government provided the blueprint for the New Deal, which swept into power following the Depression. Some of Burnham's analysis was faulty. He envisioned the U.S., Japan, and Germany as the world's power centers. World War II shattered that vision, giving way to a U.S.—U.S.S.R. bipolar world.

Sam Francis was Burnham's most able disciple. He made Burnham's worldview his own. An analysis of the managerial state was Sam's most pressing concern. Francis, too, became fascinated with power. He was also intrigued at how the managerial elites could control the minds and actions of entire populations. Television programs, Sam once complained, use soundtracks instructing a passive audience when to laugh, when to clap, when to moan, when to sigh.

The results of the managerial state? For Sam Francis, it meant a deadened, passive populace. Most important, the death of republican living. A republic, as Sam tirelessly pointed out, existed solely on a citizenry active in the life of their community. One must be involved. America? In the early 1980s, Sam and his colleagues held out some hope.

A decade later, any youthful optimism had been shattered. The road back would be a steep one. Sam's lament was recorded in the introduction to his 1993 collection, *Beautiful Losers: Essays on the Failure of American Conservatism*. Here, his prose soared to unprecedented heights. Much more was to come. The fist jumps out of the page and grabs the reader by the throat:

> If the Old Right stood for anything, it stood for the conservation of the "Old Republic" that flourished in the United States between the American War for Independence and the Great Depression and the civilization antecedents of the American republic in the history and thought of Europe and it is precisely that political construct that the managerial revolution overthrew and rendered all but impossible to restore.
>
> The Old Republic cannot be restored today because few Americans even remember it, let alone want it back, and even a realistic description, articulated by almost every theorist of republicanism from Cicero to Montesquieu, is the independence of

citizens who compose it and their commitment to a sustained active participation in its public affairs, the *res publica*. The very nature of the managerial revolution and the regime that developed from it promotes not independence, but dependency and not civic participation, but civic passivity.

The triumph was complete, seemingly permanent. The result? A failed nation:

> Today, almost the whole of American society encourages dependency and passivity, in the economy, through the continuing absorption of independent farms and businesses by multinational corporations, through ever more minute regulation by the state and through the dragooning of mass work forces in office and factory and mass consumption through advertising and public relations; in the culture, through the regimented and centralized manufacture and manipulation of thought, taste, and opinion and emotion by the mass media and educational organization; and in the state through its management of more and more dimensions of private and social existence under the color of "therapy" that does not cure, "voluntary service" that is really mandatory, and periodic "wars" against poverty, illiteracy, drugs, or other fashionable monsters, that no one ever wins.
>
> The result is an economy that does not work, a democracy that does not vote, families without fathers, classes without property, a government that passes more and more laws, a people that is more and more lawless, and a culture that neither thinks nor feels except when and what it is told or tricked to think and feel.

Samuel T. Francis and Revolution from the Middle

What did James Burnham mean to Samuel Todd Francis? Burnham was a modernist. American conservatives, under the influence of Kirk and Weaver, had a strong anti-modernist element. What's the point? The criticism of modernity is trenchant enough (i.e., the addiction to television), but doomed. Burnham accepted modernity. That wasn't the entire story. Modern or not modern, the story of history is still power.

Francis had Burnham as a model. However, Sam did not, as critics charged, want to replace a liberal big government with "big government conservatism." Social Security and Medicare reform might be dead in the water. Still, Sam called for the radical downsizing of the federal government: eliminating the Departments of Education, Energy, Commerce, Transportation, Veterans Affairs, the Interior, and the National Endowment for the Arts and the National Endowment for the Humanities. Sam supported local control of all governmental functions, especially those concerning law enforcement, education, and the redistricting process.

Freedom? Burnham was good about power. Only power negates power, he maintained. Burnham's most famous books were *The Managerial Revolution* and *The Suicide of The West*, an eye-grabbing critique of Western retreat and surrender. *The Machiavellians* (1940) may be his most important work. Not just Machiavelli, but also Alberto Mosca, Antonin Gramsci, and Victor Pareto were defenders of freedom. They alerted the citizenry to the eternal lust for power by their elites and advised how to combat it.

Power negates power. Overthrow the elites! The masses must seek power themselves. Once they attain it, they can use that power for libertarian and traditionalist ends: a government close to home and built around traditional morality. To Burnham, the end goal was a constitutional republic. And that meant a citizenry active always in the affairs of the community. That was the gospel Sam tirelessly preached over the course of his career.

James Burnham and Sam Francis wrote in different eras. In Burnham's day, the Cold War was dominant. He did not believe in global democracy. Appealing to nationalist sentiments in Eastern

Europe, Asia, and Africa was the way to prevail over Marxist-Leninism. In Sam's world, the Cold War was winding down, replaced by an anti-Western culture war, one more virulent than any foreign enemy. For Burnham, Western surrender meant retreat from empire and the Soviet challenge. For Sam, it was surrender to the Global South multi-millions. Again, power. Immigration was not about "nation of immigrants," "a better life," or Emma Lazarus's poem at the base of the Statue of Liberty. It was a means for the Republican Big Business/cheap labor and the Democratic Party/cheap vote alliance to maintain power. For both Protestant mainline and Roman Catholic churches a vehicle to seek fresh bodies for empty pews.

When Sam died in 2005, Joe Sobran eulogized his friend as the great disciple that Burnham's "brave life deserved." Chilton Williamson, Jr. did Sobran one better. Sam was Burnham's most thoughtful interpreter. Francis, however, did not just equal Burnham, he may have surpassed his mentor. In terms of true (and planned) Western surrender (the immigration invasion) and in Francis's arresting prose style, Williamson might just be correct.

5.

Beautiful Losers

SAM FRANCIS'S SIGNATURE James Burnham essay, "The Other Side of Modernism," was first published by Paul Gottfried in *The World & I* and reprinted in *Beautiful Losers: Essays on the Failure of American Conservatism*, brought out by the University of Missouri Press. The collection was Sam's report on the 1980s. For establishment conservatives, that decade was their heroic age, the economic boom coupled with the fall of the Berlin Wall. Sam's was a lonely but forceful voice of dissent. Sam Francis liked Ronald Reagan—who didn't? Upon the latter's death in 2004, Sam praised the 40th president for running a scandal-free administration, for being an amazing political success and a man truly admired by his fellow Americans.

It wasn't enough. Reagan's accomplishments as a conservative statesman, Francis added, were "pretty thin." The Soviet empire fell, not due to Reagan's policies but from Moscow's internal economic and political incoherence. At home, the size of the federal government continued to grow. The culture war was being lost. Reagan signed an immigration bill granting amnesty without achieving border security. His administration was oblivious to the rapid increase in legal immigration that transformed America into a multicultural nation.

The decade saw the extension of the Voting Rights Act and the establishment of the Martin Luther King, Jr. holiday, plus the rise of Political Correctness and anti-Western multiculturalism. A conservative decade? The GOP's defeat in the 1986 midterms proved decisive. With a Democratic Senate, the nomination of conservative favorite Robert Bork to the high court was defeated, a stinging blow.

The problem for Sam was not Reagan but conservatism itself. That ideology proclaimed that the Eighties represented morning in America, when, according to Francis, "it was far closer to the eleventh hour." "Only a Right willing and able to tell the time correctly and explain it to Americans will be able to perceive and confront the challenges Ronald Reagan missed. The Right he represented and led couldn't do that."

What was needed was right wing, not conservatism. Francis, as the 1980s wore down, had not fully articulated that replacement ideology.

Conservativism, as it entered the 1990s, was defunct. The essays in *Beautiful Losers* diagnosed that failure while offering a program of restoration. Where *did* the right go wrong? In short, they rejected any appeal to right wing populism. Conservatives tried to woo the Yale faculty. Postwar conservatism began in 1955 with the founding of William F. Buckley, Jr.'s *National Review*. Such texts as Fredrich Hayek's *The Road to Serfdom* (1944), Richard M. Weaver's *Ideas Have Consequences* (1948), and Russell Kirk's *The Conservative Mind* (1953) lit a spark. *NR* gave conservatives (and disgruntled ex-leftists) a forum to air out differences and define what the word should mean. According to Tom Fleming, Henry Regnery, the conservative publisher, advised the young Buckley not to launch a conservative periodical based in New York City. Anywhere else!

Buckley was a native of Connecticut, a man whose father had an oil-drilling empire in Mexico. The family maintained a Manhattan residence, and Buckley, with his sister Priscilla as managing editor, headquartered the magazine there rather than in Washington, where the more populist-oriented *Human Events* published. The young Buckley, as Francis noted, disdained the "cliché-ridden" idea of grassroots politics. A proud graduate (and famous critic) of Yale University, Buckley hoped to bring the intellectuals around.

Such elites had midwifed the liberal revolution. Maybe, Buckley reasoned, they could be recruited for the other side. Which never happened. In 1968, Buckley was dismayed to learn that more professors at Princeton supported the leftist comedian Dick Gregory for president than Richard Nixon. Buckley quipped that he would rather be governed by the first 100 names in the Boston phone book than by 100 professors at neighboring Harvard. Truck drivers or Ivy League?

The Buckleyites had no use for right wing populism, fearing it would lead to trade protection and a return to pre-Pearl Harbor isolationism. *NR*-style conservatism mirrored the *Wall Street Journal* editorial page: free markets and a strong military. Inspired by Richard Weaver's program of restoration—private property, combined with reverence for the past—*NR* editor Frank Meyer formulated Fusionism: traditionalists, libertarians, and anti-Soviet hawks under one big tent. In its renegade phase, *NR* vigorously attacked New Deal and Great Society spending programs. To the chagrin of later generations, it also opposed the *Brown vs. Board of Education* decision and federal civil rights legislation. It voiced muted opposition to the 1965 Immigration Bill.

During the era of Chilton Williamson Jr. as editor of *NR's* Arts and Letters section, Francis, along with Bradford, Gottfried, and Fleming contributed many reviews and essays. These included comments on the burgeoning immigration issue and skepticism over the neoconservative influence on the right, including crusades for global democracy. It didn't last long. In 1991, Williamson reportedly took a cut in pay to leave *NR* for the more hospitable pastures at *Chronicles*.

By the early Nineties, Sam Francis was a leading critic of American establishment conservatism. The concluding essay in the 1993 collection bore the same name as the book's title. "Beautiful Losers" had a unique take on things. Support for the Vietnam War was, to Francis, a fateful misstep by the Buckleyites. The war was a massive undertaking by anti-communist liberals. The Kennedy and Johnson administrations took the plunge, sending in tens of thousands and then hundreds of thousands of combat troops to beat back Ho Chi Minh's invasion of the South.

Earlier, Sam had reasoned that if America was committed to the war, it should be fought to total victory, i.e., destroying Hanoi's war-making abilities. Instead, here was another war for democracy. A coup of the anti-communist but undemocratic South Vietnamese leadership took place weeks before Kennedy's assassination. The Johnson Administration, meanwhile, offered its "TVA on the Mekong" project for the enemy. That might win them over.

Conservatives had now turned away from America First or even fighting Communism as an alien, anti-Christian ideology. Conservative support for a liberal's war, Francis maintained, was a mistake. It got the right a little pregnant with liberalism itself. Big war *is* big government. Conservatives were anti-communist. They rarely thought twice about supporting the war. The John Birch Society (JBS), a right-wing populist organization with a large membership in Reagan's Southern California base, opposed the war, preferring to fight communist infiltration at home. In 1965, the JBS was the subject of a special issue of *National Review,* one effectively expelling its members from the ranks of respectable conservatism. A decline in subscriptions made Buckley and publisher William R. Rusher wonder if they had made the right move.

Rejecting populism was a mistake. Americans weren't ready to dismantle the New Deal. Still, the right had to take on the establishment. Where to turn? Most of the essays in *Beautiful Losers* were published during the Cold War Eighties. Joe McCarthy, the Red-baiting Republican Senator from Wisconsin, was praised as a model populist. By the 1980s, McCarthy had long been cast out of polite society. An *American Spectator* article featured a cartoon of the Senator being dumped into a garbage can. In the Fifties, the right cheered on "Tail gunner Joe." Buckley's second book, co-authored with his brother-in-law L. Brett Bozell, was entitled *McCarthy and His Enemies*, a thorough defense of the embattled Wisconsinite. McCarthy died soon after his hearings on Communist infiltration ended with an official censure.

In the Eighties McCarthy enjoyed a revival. When Pat Buchanan joined the Reagan White House in 1985 as Director of Communications, the pugilistic conservative began directing hard-hitting speeches in favor of military aide to the Nicaraguan *contras*, then fighting to overthrow that nation's Marxist-Leninist Sandinista regime. Buchanan was only following Reagan's policies, but the language, blunt as ever, upset liberals greatly. In a syndicated column, Buchanan cited Dean Rusk's famous Vietnam-era question to Congress: Are you with us or against us? If the Reaganites didn't stop the Sandinistas, then San Diego would be next. A cartoon illustrated that "McCarthy" and "Buchanan" both had eight letters, two sides of the same coin. Buchanan fired back. His 1988 memoir, *Right from the Beginning,* contained a chapter "As We Remember Joe," fondly recalling the Senator who, during the Fifties, was highly popular among American Catholics. Sam was only too eager to pitch in and assist his new friend.

Why McCarthy? He was the first postwar politician to stand up to the ruling elites. The man took on liberalism root and branch. His hearings exposed, confronted, and humiliated a regnant liberalism in front of a nationally televised audience—citizens enraged by the sellout at Yalta, the loss of China, the bloody stalemate in Korea, and, yes, Communist infiltration of the U.S. government. Francis maintained:

> The great virtue of McCarthy consisted precisely in his ability to communicate to the average American what the bonds were that connected establishment liberals like [Adlai] Stevenson and crypto-Communists like [Alger] Hiss. McCarthy's rhetoric pointed directly to what they shared, isolated it, and held it up, squirming and screaming, for all the American nation to see. And what the nation saw, it did not like.

McCarthy's populism laid groundwork for the electoral victories of Richard Nixon in 1968 and Ronald Reagan in 1980. That didn't work for populism. Sam claimed that such men and their administrations were too closely connected to an elite their constituencies strongly opposed. No matter. McCarthy remains a model. In his day, the man was slandered as a liar, a fraud, a criminal, and a homosexual. McCarthy gave as good as he got. The man was a fighter. As always, the elites are on one side, the populists on the other:

> The American Right, if it is serious about wanting to preserve the nation and its social fabric and political culture in any recognizable form, must continue to embrace Joe McCarthy and the kind of militant popular, anti-liberal, and anti-establishment movement that he was the first to express on a national scale.

Another model? Back to the heartland. The *Beautiful Losers* collection included a glowing essay on Willmoore Kendall, the firebrand essayist who was a vital force during *NR*'s early years, only to have a falling out with Buckley and other editors. (For Kendall, feuds were a way of life.) Kendall was a child prodigy, a native of Oklahoma, the son of a blind Methodist preacher. He published his first book, *How to Play Baseball*, at the tender age of 15. His teaching career took him to Yale, where the young William F. Buckley, Jr. was one of his students. Kendall feuded also with the Yale faculty who gladly bought out his contract so he could teach elsewhere. Kendall settled down at the conservative University of Dallas, where he met a premature end in 1966 at age 62. Disgusted with the East Coast elites, Kendall proudly described himself as an "Appalachian to Rockies patriot."

Buckley may have disdained the grassroots, but Kendall exerted a strong influence on *NR* editors. Burnham, as noted, declared that Middle America conservatives would bring down the Soviet Empire. Frank Meyer hailed the heartland as "the last stand of Western civilization." More important, William Rusher often escaped the offices at East 35th Street, attempting to form a nationwide populist third party, whose dream ticket for 1976 would have been Ronald Reagan and George Wallace. That went nowhere, so Rusher boosted the populist preachers of the religious right: Rev. Jerry Falwell, Rev. Pat Robertson, and Rev. James Robinson. Kendall was a forerunner to Donald Warren's Middle American Radicals. He echoed McCarthy's anti-establishment rhetoric. Francis wrote:

> The characteristic of Kendall's political thought is his unrelenting defense of the historic mainstream of the heartland, of American society against a radical and basically un-American establishment, and the value of his ideas for political conservatism today is that they offer a framework for attacking the establishment.

There was some surprise in this essay. The paleoconservatism that was forming in the mid-1980s turned out to be pessimistic. Burnham was a pessimist, Kendall an optimist. Such writers as Buchanan, Fleming, and Francis became known for a gloomy conservatism that contrasted starkly with Reaganite optimism. How can gloom and doom win over a nation that from the beginning has been devoted to progress upon progress, victory upon victory? Kendall was a Happy Warrior for the Right. The cast of Kendall's conservatism was essentially optimistic, and he shunned the thought of pessimistic conservatives who saw liberalism, retreat, and decadence as the dominant forces in the United States and the West.

In *Beautiful Losers,* Francis did not champion any candidate or a third party. Before Buchanan ran against George H.W. Bush in the 1992 Republican Party primaries, Francis held little hope for that year's presidential prospects. Conservatives needed to build a popular front that could translate later into political victors. Francis laid out the battle plan:

> Instead of the uselessness of a Diogenes' search for an honest presidential candidate or a Fabian quest for a career in the bureaucracy, a Middle America right should begin working in and with schools, churches,

clubs, women's groups, youth organizations, civic and professional associations, local government, the military and police forces, and even labor unions to create a radicalized Middle American consciousness. Only when this kind of infrastructure of cultural hegemony is developed can a Middle America Right seek meaningful political power without conditions with the Left and bargaining with the regime.

An active citizenry might awaken the slumbering Republican elephant into taking a populist turn. In the years ahead, California's anti-illegal immigration Proposition 197, the Buchanan and Ross Perot campaigns, the Tea Party rebellion, the Donald Trump presidency, and the parental opposition to Critical Race Theory (CRT) were examples of Sam Francis-style politics. Would the elephant ever get the two-by-four induced message?

Critics and friends, such as Peter Gemma, consider *Beautiful Losers* to be Sam's finest volume. It's hard to argue with that. The prose is learned but angry and uncompromising. The author gives no quarter to liberals and conservatives alike. *Beautiful Losers* was mostly ignored by the conservative media, something Sam expected. It was reviewed in several publications, including *The Detroit News*, whose reviewer praised Francis as a "skilled prose stylist; his essays are often a pleasure to read for that reason alone." The reception to one essay illustrated the near-impossible climb Sam Francis-style conservatism would face.

Beautiful Losers was published by Beverly Jarrett, the intrepid editor of the University of Missouri Press. During her tenure Jarrett, the wife of novelist William Mills, was sympathetic to the Old Right's political and literary tradition. In addition to Sam Francis, Jarrett published M.E. Bradford, Tom Fleming, Clyde Wilson, Paul Gottfried, Marion Montgomery, George Garrett, Cleanth Brooks, and Andrew Lytle. The latter's 1993 essay, *Kristin: A Reading*, a study of Sigrid Undset's *Kristin Lavransdatter* trilogy, was published when the author was 91 years old.

Beautiful Losers, however, was the first and only Sam Francis volume Missouri would bring out. Even more controversial than the McCarthy essay was "The Cult of Dr. King," critical of the Martin Luther King, Jr. holiday. Rumor had it that the press faculty advisors took one look at the essay and were mighty displeased. That was it for Sam and Columbia, Missouri.

The King essay originally appeared in a 1988 number of *Chronicles*, one grimly titled "Ethnic Conflict," featuring reports from such trouble spots as Northern Ireland and the Balkans. In 1983, when the King holiday was approved by Congress, Pat Buchanan and William F. Buckley, Jr. wrote columns critical of the man, even though Buckley, who had a long friendship with Ronald Reagan, agreed with the former's decision to sign it into law. The holiday came into being surrounding the 20th anniversary of King's "I Have A Dream" 1963 speech pushing for passage of federal civil rights laws. It was first proposed in 1968 by Rep. John Conyers (D—MI) only days after King's assassination on April 4, 1968. For years, the legislation went nowhere. President Jimmy Carter pitched the holiday during his State of the Union addresses. Neither Republicans nor large numbers of conservative Democrats were interested.

In 1980, while running for re-election, Carter claimed that if Reagan were elected, the holiday would never become law. Reagan indeed was opposed to the holiday even after the anniversary of the 1963 march came and went. But the Democratic Congress approved the King holiday bill. (Richard Cheney, then a congressman from Wyoming and future Vice President, opposed it.) The Senate, controlled by Republicans, also went along. The revenge of Reagan's rivals? Both Majority Leader Howard Baker (R—TN) and his successor, Robert J. Dole (R—KS) ran unsuccessfully against Reagan in the 1980 primaries. Dole, for instance, received only one percent of the vote in the New Hampshire primary. Baker, with the help of liberal Republican Charles Mathias (R—MD) and Democrat Edward M. Kennedy (D—MASS) easily achieved passage of the bill. Misgivings aside, Reagan, citing "the gravity of the moment," signed the bill into law.

Joining Senator Jesse Helms (R-NC) in opposition were such solons as Barry Goldwater (R-AZ) and Steve Symms (R-ID). King had been highly critical of Goldwater. In 1964, King declared that that there were "elements of Hitlerism" in the Goldwater campaign, despite the latter's service, in his forties, to the United States Air Force during World War II. The support of the King holiday by Buckley and Reagan represented a 180-degree turn by the right. In the late 1960s, as King's rhetoric became more heated, Buckley criticized those excesses, including King's willingness to break the law. Such arguments no longer mattered. Reagan signed the bill. That was good enough. Opposing the holiday would mean ostracization from the leftist-dominated New York-Washington chattering classes. Establishment Conservatives wanted to be part of that world.

Jesse Helms became the face of the opposition. The October 3, 1983 speech he gave on the Senate floor was written by Sam Francis. That year was fraught with great peril between the two superpowers. Helms's speech focused on King's Communist connections. In the post-1917 world, it was not unusual for prominent black Americans such as Paul Robeson to attach themselves to Communist-oriented groups. Communists promised equality and even proposed a "Black Belt" nation in the Deep South. The old America preferred the Booker T. Washington pro-capitalist approach. With World War II and de-colonization abroad, the push for civil rights at home was greatly strengthened.

What Helms found most offensive was King's associates at a time when war was raging in far-off Vietnam. Two of them, Stanley Levinson and Jack O'Dell, were both members of the Communist Party of the United States (CPUSA). King, in the 1950s, had attended the Highlander Folk School in Monteagle, Tennessee, that Helms said was a pro-Communist training school. Levinson, Helms maintained, influenced King's opposition to the Vietnam War. That opposition, Helms charged, "was not predicated on what King believed to be the best interests of the United States, but on sympathy for the North Vietnamese Communist regime and on an essentially Marxist and anti-American ideological view of U.S. foreign policy."

Strong stuff. And to no avail. The speech was attacked by New York Senator Daniel Patrick Moynihan (D–NY) as a "packet of filth." New Jersey solon Bill Bradley compared the address to the worst excesses of "Bull" Connor. King's Communist associates were deemed irrelevant then and more so now, especially since the Cold War is long over.

Sam's essay observed that criticism of the holiday or the man was now off-limits. Karen Collins, a Silver Springs, Maryland music schoolteacher, was placed on administrative leave and forced to take a "human relations" course after she told students that King "had been a communist supporter and had communist friends." Sam quoted one Vincent Harding who praised King, not for his moderation, but for the radical stand the former had taken, *circa* 1968:

> King was calling for and leading disobedience campaigns against the unjust war in Vietnam. He was encouraging young men to refuse to serve in the military, challenging them not to support America's anti-Communist crusades, which were really destroying the hopes of poor nonwhite peoples everywhere. This Martin Luther King was calling for the radical redistribution of wealth and political power in American society as a way to provide food, clothing, shelter, medical care, jobs, education, and hope for all of our country's people.

Above all, American history, to Sam, was at stake. By the late Eighties, the culture war against America's Western inheritance was in full swing. Central was the campaign against Sam's beloved Southland concerning its Confederate heritage: opposition to Confederate flags, monuments, and statues and even to calling a high school football team "The Rebels" and to playing "Dixie" at public events. That wasn't all. Sam firmly believed the King holiday was an impetus for both anti-American and anti-Western activity:

> The Martin Luther King holiday was the first and most important instance of this [anti-Western] trend but by no means the last. The King holiday was merely the legitimizing agent of the attacks on other symbols that have occurred since. Attacks on the Confederate flag and Southern white symbols are now commonplace, but the Alamo in San Antonio is another traditional white symbol that is also under attack—by Hispanics. The Custer battlefield in Montana now celebrates the Indian victory, although what is historically memorable about the battle of the Little Big Horn is not the victory of a thousand Indians over a small American cavalry detachment but the defeat of whites at the hands of non-whites.

In 1987, the revolution moved to a new phase: frontal assault on the Western canon. Francis skewered the pivotal "hey, hey, ho, ho, Western civ has got to go" rally at Stanford University. Down with the classics, up with W.E.B. Du Bois, Frantz Fanon, Herbert Marcuse, and Karl Marx:

> Whatever merits such writers might have over the ancient, medieval, and modern classics of the West, it should be clear that the alternative curriculum was intended as part of the radical reconstruction of the American mind and the extirpation of the philosophical roots of Western predominance. The demand for the change at Stanford, according to news reports, was led by black, Hispanic, and Asian students who denounced the traditional curriculum as a "year-long class in racism."

For Francis it was all of one piece:

> The point is not that the establishment of the King holiday makes the extirpation of the traditional symbols of American and Western civilization inevitable—anti-American and anti-Western movements founded on militant egalitarian universalism are powerful forces and would make gains regardless of the holiday—but that, once the United States, through its national government, chose to adopt Dr. King as an official hero, neither the American people nor their leaders had any legitimate grounds to resist the logic and dynamic of such forces and the radical reconstruction of American society that is implicit in them.

Old Right conservatives waxed bitterly over Ronald Reagan's reluctant decision in signing the holiday. Reagan remained uncomfortable with the entire process. "We'll know in 2027," Reagan snapped at a reporter when asked if King's alleged Communist connections were true. (In that year the Federal Bureau of Investigation's King files, were set to be made public.) A small furor erupted and Reagan, facing a re-election bid, stepped back from his response. To Sam and other conservatives, that represented a betrayal. After all, Southern conservatives in 1976 singlehandedly saved Reagan's political career. After losing five straight primaries to President Ford, Reagan rebounded to win a decisive victory in North Carolina and later in both Texas and Georgia. Reagan eventually lost to Ford, but he solidified his front runner status for 1980.

Sam Francis proved as prophetic as ever. In his 1981 inaugural address, President Reagan invoked the greatness of three men—Washington, Jefferson and Lincoln—whose monuments define the city's landscape. By 1981, Washington had been knocked down a few pegs. In 1968, the U.S. Congress, under pressure from the American Auto Association (AAA), eliminated Washington's

February 22 birthdate as a national holiday, turning into a three-day weekend. In 1971, President Nixon ended that practice, turning Washington's and Lincoln's February 12 birthday into a meaningless "President's Day."

In the late 1990s, the New Orleans public school board renamed a George Washington Elementary School. Two decades later, with the culture war raging onward, a mural of Washington in a San Francisco high school was, following student protests, painted over. In 2021, that same school board voted to rename schools named for Washington, Jefferson, and Lincoln, plus those for James A. Garfield, Theodore Roosevelt, and Franklin D. Roosevelt, all before backing down under public outcry.

Also, by the late Nineties, the Jefferson-Sally Hemmings hoax was given new life, dug up to protect the scandal-ridden Bill Clinton presidency. Connor Cruise O'Brien's 1996 book, *The Long Affair: Thomas Jefferson and the French Revolution 1785-1800*, explicitly tried to knock Jefferson from his pedestal, as did an essay in *The Atlantic*. Washington and Jefferson labor under their slave-owning pasts. There is Jefferson's equality clause in the Declaration of Independence—and his actual life. Lincoln, as the Great Emancipator, fares the best. But the 16th president isn't home free. Since the late 1980s, American culture has been on a tear against white males. That includes Abraham Lincoln. The latter became a victim of anti-white-male paranoia. In far-left Berkeley and San Francisco, public schools for Lincoln have been renamed. The change in Berkeley remains permanent.

The New South had room for both Robert E. Lee and Booker T. Washington. Throughout the decades, American presidents as different as Dwight D. Eisenhower, Ronald Reagan, and Donald Trump have, for the sake of Southern audiences, sung Lee's praises. On the heels of Charleston, Charlottesville, and Minneapolis, Lee has replaced Benedict Arnold as the villain in the American story. Monuments and statues of Lee were attacked and removed, public schools and highways renamed. The same was true of John C. Calhoun, Jefferson Davis, and Stonewall Jackson. With Lee, liberals and conservatives finally found common ground. On the heels of the Jefferson hit job, *The Atlantic*, in 2017, did the same, attacking the notion of a kindly General Lee. In 2020, *National Review* followed suit with its own negative essay by Allen Guezlo. The *New York Times*, *New York*, *New Yorker*, *Los Angeles Times*, and *Claremont Review*, among numerous other publications, piled on.

Sam Francis's views on the Civil War and the South's defeat were not as apocalyptic as his fellow rightists. In a 1996 *Southern Partisan* interview, Sam expressed skepticism towards the South's desire to go to war with the more powerful Union Army. It was a war the South could not win, much less should have fought. Francis was a Lincoln critic. His friendships with Bradford and Wilson mattered. In an address at a Claremont Institute symposium, Sam made the case against Lincoln. The man, Francis declared, was an "incompetent" who could not see that the Deep South was serious about both secession and if need be, war. Lincoln had no plan to deal with the secessionists. His decision to re-supply Fort Sumter was, to Sam, the "greatest blunder in American history," one that Lincoln's Secretary of War, Secretary of State, Secretary of the Interior, Secretary of the Navy, and senior general all advised against. The Confederacy, now joined by the mid-South, doubled in size, wealth, and power, while gaining Robert E. Lee and Stonewall Jackson, its two greatest captains.

Francis did not declare Lincoln to be a revolutionary. It was never the man's intention to overthrow the old Republic. Lincoln, to Sam, was an old-fashioned Whig: economic affluence, economic equality, yes; social equality, no. Francis criticized Lincoln for making Economic Man the center of any administration. Sam's views coincided with Mel Bradford, who also acknowledged that the "sad man from Illinois" was never an egalitarian.

Unlike Bradford and Wilson, Francis did not believe the demise of the American republic was a result of the war. The period from 1776 to 1932 was his model for republican governance. America's entry into World War II was where the Liberal Revolution achieved decisive victory. Still, the Confederacy was part of Francis's bloodlines. Can't say no to that! Francis confronted the Left on all fronts: an essay defending Thomas Jefferson in the *New American*, plus numerous columns on the Confederate flag issue. Left and right *had* come together. For America to live, Robert E. Lee must die. King's birthday is on January 19. Lee's, as it turns out, is on January 21. Can the 21st century South have both General Lee and Dr. King? As Bradford observed, he who controls the past dictates the future.

Sam manfully fought a rear-guard action. By 1990, the Left was mopping the floor with their conservative patsies. Sam, meanwhile, was a lonely figure. At times, it seemed that he was fighting a one-man uphill battle against the forces of planned disintegration.

6.

America First

BEAUTIFUL LOSERS established Sam as an authoritative voice of an emerging paleoconservatism. In the mid-1980s his career, due to tragic circumstances, was in turmoil. East's 1980 senate win was a slim one. Next up was 1986, an off-year election favorable to the Democrats. A 1985 poll showed East running well. East wanted that re-election bid. However, it was not to be. East's health began to fail. A case of hypothyroidism flared up. In late 1985, he told GOP operatives that he was simply not up for the 1986 campaign. East fell into despair. His depression worsening, East, on June 29, 1986, committed suicide. The loss to the right was grievous. Helms was more dramatic. East was more articulate. He was fearless in the defense of right-wing conservatism.

In the early 1980s, East had been polishing up the before-mentioned *The American Conservative Movement: The Intellectual Founders*, a collection of previously published essays, to be brought by Regnery, the venerable conservative house. East publicly thanked Sam Francis for his assistance in bringing the book to press. The jacket copy contained a melancholy salute to the late Senator. "At the time of his death, he was considered the most *intelligent* man in the United States Senate." Which he was. No other Senator could publish a book with the breadth and scope of East's posthumous manuscript.

A bereaved Francis, now 39 years old, had to weigh his options. He would not stay on with James Broyhill, the Republican congressman chosen by Governor James Martin to fill East's seat. Francis briefly considered a position at the National War College. Sam might have preferred academia to the thankless challenge of trying to knock sense into "the Stupid Party," but he was a writer now. The essays published in *The World & I* were most timely. That glossy publication was a major supplement to the *Washington Times*.

In the early 1980s, William Cheshire, the *Times'* editorial page editor, sought out Clyde Wilson, a former journalist and fellow Tar Heel, for an editorial page position. Clyde was already teaching at the University of South Carolina. He had been publishing for up to a decade. Plus, he had a young family in Columbia and was on a tenure track at USC. He couldn't drop that job and re-locate. He recommended the young Sam Francis for the post. That didn't happen at first. By 1987, however, Sam was an ideal fit for the *Times*. Anti-communism —and not the culture wars—was then the overriding focus of the conservative media.

With the *Times,* Sam was able to stay in the Washington area, eventually settling in Seabrook, Maryland, a suburban area north of the city. At the *Times*, Sam had allies, notably R. Cort Kirkwood, Fran Combs, and Mary Lou Forbes. In time, he would gain enemies. Throughout the Eighties, the *Times* was on a roll, a classic example of being in the right place at the right time. For decades, the *Washington Star* had served as a conservative afternoon counterweight to the all-powerful *Washington Post*. The *Star* hung on for years, folding finally in 1981. Picking up the pieces was the eccentric Sun Myung Moon, an anti-communist South Korean who filled the need for a conservative daily in Ronald Reagan's Washington by funding the *Washington Times*.

In 1982, the *Washington Times* hit the stands, having Arnold de Bourgrave, a charismatic and well-traveled Austrian journalist, as its editor. Sam was a good soldier. No other writer at the *Times* could match Sam as a blunt stylist and well-read conservative intellectual. Proof came with Sam being the only Timesman to win two editorial writing awards from the Newspapers Guild of

America. As important, Sam came through in a time of crisis. In 1987, Cheshire, after a fight with ownership, resigned. So did other editors.

The editorial page staff had been obliterated. Francis stayed on. He was tossed into the fire, taking Cheshire's place as emergency editorial page editor. Ownership had to appreciate that. Sam shepherded the page through that upheaval. The job was only temporary. Once a new editor was named, Sam resumed his old duties: writing three unsigned editorials a week, editing copy, and in time writing his twice-weekly syndicated column. Sam's friends were disappointed that he wasn't named permanent editorial page editor. After all, Sam had steered the paper through a difficult time, one that proved decisive for its immediate survival. As Francis would learn in the years ahead, no good deed goes unpunished.

By the late 1980s, Sam had two publishing homes: the *Washington Times* and a monthly column in *Chronicles,* now edited by Tom Fleming. The *Chronicles* column was called "Powers and Principalities," from the *Book of Ephesians* (6:12): "For we wrestle not against flesh and blood, but against principalities, against powers, against the rulers of the darkness of this world, against spiritual wickedness in high *places.*"

Sam would fight the devil—from the right, of course. In 1991, after five years of service and two distinguished writing awards, Sam was given his own syndicated column, distributed nationally by the Tribune Syndicate. Friends hoped he would be given permanent control of the editorial page. What a revolution that could spark! This was not to be. The *Times* was conservative. It was *not* right-wing. Having Sam running its (hopefully) influential editorial page was never a possibility.

Fleming and Gottfried were Sam's loyal allies. He was not alone in Washington. His position at the *Times* seemed secure. With his friendship with Patrick J. Buchanan, however, Francis was now in the orbit of the most accomplished, profound, and popular pundit the much-ballyhooed conservative movement has ever produced.

When did Buchanan and Francis become friends? In 1981, when Sam went to work for Senator East, Buchanan was established as the leading voice on the populist right, complementing the more urbane views of Buckley and George F. Will. His radio talk show with Tom Braden of *Eight Is Enough* fame morphed into *Crossfire,* a popular, award-winning nightly half-hour slam-bang cable television affair, where Buchanan "from the right" dominated. When in 1985 Buchanan took a significant pay cut to work as President Reagan's Director of Communications, conservatives were delighted to have one of their own giving forceful advice to the president.

As the 1988 election approached, Buchanan was being talked about as a presidential candidate. In 1987, the man gave a rip-roaring speech in front of the White House, defending the president as the Iran-Contra scandal broke. Momentum was building. Reporters urged Pat to run. ("Get it, Pat. It's so boring!") So, too, did numerous right-wing operatives. Buchanan reportedly had a dream where he was the target of an assassination attempt. He said "no" to a 1988 run, even though the possibility of a future campaign existed.

With his opposition to the Gulf War, Buchanan, just as quickly, became ostracized on the respectable right. Old friends abandoned him. Concerning Buchanan's America First platform, Fred Barnes crowed: "You guys aren't a wing of the party. You're not even a feather!" Buchanan sought out allies. East and Helms were two of Pat's favorite senators. Buchanan's column ran above the fold on the *Times'* op-ed page. He was also a faithful *Chronicles* reader. Buchanan offered positive blurbs for the Rockford Institute fundraising letters.

Sam, in turn, admired Buchanan's hard-hitting prose and uncompromising stands. When Buchanan and *New York Times* columnist A.M. Rosenthal got into a public feud over Pat's comment that the only people banging the war drums for a 1991 war with Iraq were "the Israeli defense ministry and its amen corner in the United States," Sam, along with Joe Sobran and Murray Rothbard, sprang to Pat's defense.

Buchanan was born in 1938, Sam in 1947. There was a generational difference. By 1990, Buchanan was the most controversial polemicist in America. Sam was just beginning to make his impact felt. Big brother, little brother? Something else? I recall a conversation with Sam where he told me that he had joined Pat and Shelley (Buchanan's wife) to watch the movie version of the musical *Chicago*. Imagine the scene, Sam tagging along with Pat and Shelley at a suburban movie complex. A filial attachment? Maybe so. Pat needed allies. He needed friendship. As did Sam. With Pat Buchanan as a booster, Sam had graduated into the top tier of American journalism.

Buchanan and Francis were comrades-in-arms. Barnes and other establishment conservatives, including Buckley, rejected any notion that America First could make a comeback in national politics. Did 1990 America remember America First? Probably not, but the media sure did. Buchanan was now the towering figure of American conservatism. In the pre-Limbaugh, pre-Internet age, Buchanan was on the air nightly, as opposed to only once-a-week appearances by both Buckley (*Firing Line*) and George Will (*This Week with David Brinkley*).

In the December 1991 number of *Chronicles*, Francis presented the duo's America First manifesto. The essay was blunt and far-reaching. What should America First, circa 1991, entail? This was a far different nation than had existed in 1940: more suburban, more affluent, more hedonistic, multicultural, far more liberal. America First rejected democracy promotion or the defense of human rights in foreign affairs. It sought to protect the historic American nation from all enemies foreign or domestic. America First, ultimately, would be just as much a cultural expression as a political position. Some key planks from the Sam Francis platform:

- Office-holders and candidates for office should be expected to commit themselves to the principle of the national sovereignty and independence of the United States. No treaty should be concluded or ratified that compromises or dilutes national sovereignty or requires changes in U.S. law and policy contrary to the Constitution.

- There must be a geopolitical definition of a secure area beyond the borders of the United States into which foreign powers would not be allowed to intrude militarily. Pat Buchanan has suggested confining this area to Central America, the Caribbean and the northern littoral of South America. I would expand it to literally hemispheric dimensions, extending from the North Pole to the South and from the Greenwich Meridian to the International Date Line.

- The United States should maintain an adequate standing military force to (a) protect its territory and citizens within the hemispheric perimeter and (b) mount rapid and effective punitive and rescue missions outside the perimeter against aggressive powers as needed. The right to vote should be contingent upon fulfilling the military obligations of the citizens and this is consistent with the classical republican ideal of a citizens' militia.

- There must be a clear recognition of congressional supremacy in foreign affairs. Every long-term or far-reaching foreign or military commitment must have the explicit approval of Congress.

- No U.S. troops will be committed to combat in the absence of congressional approval and unless military victory is the publicly stated goal.

- Lobbying on behalf of a foreign government or country should be made a federal crime.

- "America First" implies a nationalistic ethic that transcends the preferences and interests of the individual or the interest group and involves local, state, or federal government action. The ethic of America First ought to inform the total cultural life of the nation and to be the foundation of our social and cultural identity no less than of our politics and national policies.

Francis returned to the trade and immigration issues, now looming larger than ever:

- America First trade and immigration policies should recognize that we owe duties to ourselves and our compatriots before we owe anything to other peoples and restrictions on immigration, free trade, and technology transfer should be debated and framed in terms of our national identity.

- Immigration from other countries and cultures that are incompatible with and indigestible to the Euro-American cultural core of the United States should be prohibited, current border controls should be rigorously enforced, illegal aliens already here should be rounded up and deported, and employers who hire them should be prosecuted and punished.

What did Buchanan and Francis plan to do with their America First platform? They needed allies. Both were friends with Sobran, Fleming, and Rothbard. They needed publicity. Buchanan's fame would make that an easy task. What else? Press conferences? Lectures on college campuses? The endless rounds of radio and television talk shows? Public demonstrations? A newsletter? A politician or two expressing support?

In 1988, Buchanan did not run for president. Four years later, a different story. Buchanan was a critic of the Bush Administration. Opposition to the Gulf War was central. There were other issues. In 1991, trouble had brewed over affirmative action. In 1989, the Supreme Court had ruled against two such programs, one in Richmond, Virginia, the other in Brooklyn, New York. The Democratic Congress reacted, approving legislation to overturn such decisions. President Bush initially resisted before caving in, signing a pro-affirmative bill into law.

Buchanan wrote a standard column criticizing the GOP and its guilt-ridden ways. Pat's sister, Bay, a former U.S. Treasurer and loyal Reaganite, phoned her brother and delivered the blunt message: "Pat, get in." That was all Bay's older brother needed. It was now off to New Hampshire where an endorsement by the powerful *Manchester Union-Leader* awaited the rookie candidate. First, however, was a big meeting at the Buchanan homestead in McLean, Virginia. It had happened before. In 1987, while contemplating that same run, conservative activists crowded the living room. One of them, Tom Ellis, a longtime Jesse Helms ally who had engineered Reagan's upset of Gerald Ford in the 1976 North Carolina GOP presidential primary, gave an impassioned speech, decrying a Soviet beach head in Nicaragua, implying that only a President Buchanan could reverse such ominous gains on America's doorstep.

That was 1987. Four years later, a different world was aborning. The Berlin Wall was down. The Nicaraguan Sandinistas were out of power. The Cold War was over. Far greater threats were already in motion. America's border remained unprotected. Blue collar jobs were hurtling overseas. The "hey, hey, ho, ho, Western Civ has got to go" chant had replaced the Evil Empire as the hard right's new enemy. Someone who wasn't at the 1987 confab was front and center at the 1991 get-together.

Sam Francis now stood on the brink of national recognition. When Buchanan ran in 1992, he instructed his syndicate to pick up Sam's column as a replacement. Francis considered Buchanan as the most heroic public intellectual of our time. Pat, in turn, viewed Sam as a younger—and highly effective—advocate for America First. There was one key difference between the two, namely the word itself, *conservative*. What the heck did that mean anymore? A veteran of the Goldwater, Nixon, and Reagan movements, Buchanan still believed. Francis rejected the word and its spokesmen. There was a generational divide.

In his essay, "From Household to Nation," Sam recalled that the get-together contained the usual number of "hangers-on, direct mail artists, fund-raising whiz kids, marketing and PR czars and the rest of the crew that never fail to show up on the campaign doorstep to guzzle someone's else liquor and pocket other people's money." All, to Francis, were as obsolete as the Republican Party. When Sam had Pat's ear, he made his case:

> These people are defunct, I told him. You don't need them, and you're better off without them. Go to New Hampshire and call yourself a patriot, a nationalist, an America Firster, but don't even use the word 'conservative.' It doesn't mean anything anymore.

For now, however, Buchanan would remain a party man. Sam was disappointed:

> Pat listened, but I can't say he took my advice. By making his bed with the Republicans, he opens himself to charges that he's not a "true" party man or a "true" conservative, constrains his chances for victory by the need to massage Republicans whose highest goal is to win elections, and only dilutes and deflects the radicalism of the message he and his Middle American Revolution have to offer.
>
> The sooner we hear that message loudly and clearly, without distractions from Conservatism. Inc. and the Stupid Party, the sooner Middle America will be

able to speak with an authentic voice and the sooner we can get on with conserving the nation from the dominations and powers that are destroying it.

Buchanan cherished the conservatism of the 1960s, when the crew-cut right squared off against the long-haired lefties. To Francis, that world was gone. Buchanan's mission was two-fold. "In order to get our party back, we have to get our movement back," he had declared. To which Francis might respond: What movement? What party? With his usual eloquence, M.E. Bradford maintained that to be a "conservative" was meaningless, "it is to perpetuate the outrageous," conserving the reigning liberal regime.

For Sam Francis, no turning back. Right-wing or nothing. In early 1993 he drove home the same point, this time in the company of another distinguished conservative. As Paul Gottfried tells it, Buchanan once again invited a circle of friends to McLean, this time to discuss the formation of The American Cause, a political action committee. At the meeting was Russell Kirk and his wife Annette. Pat and Sam both read and admired the great Kirk. Author of the 1953 landmark tome, *The Conservative Mind*, Kirk single handedly made *conservatism* a respectable intellectual term. The Anglo-American tradition, Kirk maintained, was just that, exemplified by such leaders as Benjamin Disraeli, John Adams, and John C. Calhoun, plus poets T.S. Eliot and Robert Frost. None were progressive. All were conservative and, in some cases, downright reactionary.

At the meeting, Sam was seated in the living room near the Kirks. Sam was outspoken. He also enjoyed being impish. "I am not a conservative," he said in the company of the intellectual founder of the movement, "but a man of the Right, perhaps the far Right." Kirk, according to Gottfried, said nothing. Who was Sam Francis to the august Kirk? Gottfried added that Annette Kirk was annoyed, but she, too, declined the bait. Kirk read Buchanan. Did he read Sam Francis? On the inside picture page to Kirk's posthumously published memoir, *The Sword of Imagination,* the author is seated at his desk, diligently typing away. To his side are several books, including Donald Davidson's history of the Tennessee River and Sam's own *Power and History.*

In December 1991, Buchanan did go to New Hampshire. And he did call himself a conservative. It was a far different conservatism than the Goldwater or Reagan variety. Pat trumpeted America First: "No" to free trade and unnecessary foreign wars; "Yes" to border security, along with the usual robust pro-life message. Buchanan gained such momentum that President Bush had to make a reluctant visit to the Granite State. No matter. Buchanan shocked the punditry, scoring 37 percent of the vote to 53 percent for Bush.

Buchanan's strong showing propelled H. Ross Perot, Texas billionaire and champion of Vietnam Prisoners of War, to jump into the race. Drawing large crowds everywhere, the folksy Texan quickly pulled to a solid lead over both President Bush and the presumed Democrat nominee, Arkansas Governor Bill Clinton. Perot was Buchananite on trade and foreign policy. He avoided the immigration issue and was pro-choice on abortion, while declaring on the "Larry King Show" that "every life is precious."

Buchanan, now losing to Bush in the primaries, praised the Perot insurgency, while reiterating his disagreement with the Texan on abortion. In the fall election, Perot, after dropping out of the race in the summer, then climbing back in during the fall, received an impressive 19 percent of the vote. Fiscal conservatives abandoned Bush for Perot. Clinton won the presidency in 1992 with 43 percent, but the pro-life vote stayed with Bush. If Perot had been pro-life, who knows?

Francis supported Buchanan's run. He praised his friend as the one candidate who had something concrete to say to working-class voters and for saying it well. Sam was amused by Perot, but not fully supportive. The latter did not have the temperament for politics. Perot initially dropped out of the '92 race after being lambasted for addressing an NAACP convention in Nashville, claiming that "you people" were the first ones hurt when the economy took a dive. Such comments were hardly racist, but the man felt overwhelmed.

The next year, Perot blew his early lead in the polls after delivering angry exchanges with Vice President Al Gore during a NAFTA debate on that same Larry King program. Perot, to Sam, was a high-stakes businessman out of his depth in politics. His third-party run, however, was far preferable to either the Dems or the GOP.

By August, Buchanan's 1992 campaign wasn't over. He received a prime time speaking slot at the GOP convention in Houston. There, he delivered his famous "culture war" address, one that horrified GOP politicos but excited the capacity crowd. Sam liked Pat's "brilliant and moving" speech, but he did see flaws in it:

> Pat Buchanan endorsed President Bush and offered such reasons as he could think to support him. This was the weakest part of Mr. Buchanan's address; he was obliged to dwell on the president's commendable personal war record of some fifty years ago as opposed to the still mysterious conduct of Mr. Clinton when he was of draft age in the Vietnam era. The contrast in this respect between the two candidates may well indicate an important distinction of character between them, but it's stretching to claim that the two men's performance or non-performance in two different kinds of wars offered a compelling reason for enthusiastic support of the former fighter pilot.

Sam had a point. Vietnam became an unpopular war. Both parties would nominate Vietnam veterans as their standard bearers (Al Gore and John Kerry for the Democrats, John McCain for the Republicans.) None would win the presidency. Clinton's draft-dodging was never a major issue, any more than Dan Quayle's and George W. Bush's National Guard service. Likewise, the talk of "family values" was equally meaningless. By 1992, the Democrats, as Sam observed, were influenced by "homosexuals, abortionists [and] womanologists." They faced off against a supine GOP that had no desire to overturn Leftist gains in the culture war.

Nineteen ninety-two was another important year for Sam Francis. Through Buchanan's spirited run, America First had thrown a scare into the political elite. Moreover, Pat, as noted, had appointed Sam as his replacement for the former's popular syndicated column. Pat's column ran in 500 newspapers. Did Sam's dispatches appear in each one? Francis was considerably more controversial than even his older friend. Either way, Sam now had a faithful nationwide audience. Now his byline reached millions. That spike in fame possibly inspired Beverly Jarrett to solicit the *Beautiful Losers* essay collection for publication.

The year also represented a significant milestone in the history of the Republican Party, one that it has never recovered from. Consider the seismic shifts. In 1968, once-stable America was falling apart. Violence abroad, violence at home. In 1964, Lyndon Johnson won a 44-state landslide with 61 percent of the vote. Four years later, Johnson was knocked out of the race by an unknown Senator from Minnesota. Johnson's vice president, Hubert Humphrey, garnered only 42 percent of the popular vote in a three-man race.

From 1968 to 1988, the GOP presidential nominee averaged 53 percent of the popular vote. The Democratic counterpart struggled home with an average of 43 percent. A landslide advantage for the GOP. From 1992 to 2012, a similar six election cycle—and a different story. Now, the GOP average was 45 percent. The Dems' upped their total to 48 percent.

What happened? From 1968 to 1988, American politics was dominated by the Cold War struggle. After Vietnam, Americans had little stomach to put the Democrats in power. Kennedy and Johnson had plunged America into Vietnam. Nixon painstakingly withdrew the forces. The Cold War over, the culture wars now dominated. America was just as libertine in the 1960s, '70s and '80s as it is today. By the 1990s, however, there were no Soviet missiles aimed at America. The George H.W. Bush presidency, especially the popular-turned-unpopular Persian Gulf War, was the turning point.

Francis notably coined a label for the Republican Party that caught on and was often used by others—"the Stupid Party." The Democrats were "the Evil Party." The Republicans were "the Stupid Party" because they always retreated and lost on their issues.

For years, such New Right activists as Richard Viguerie and Howard Phillips dreaded a Bush presidency. "Poppy" proved them right. He reneged on his no new taxes pledge. His war against Iraq over Kuwait was wildly popular at first. As 1992 approached, those approval numbers sank considerably. Bush supported increases in legal immigration. He did nothing to secure the border. Then there was the abortion issue. In 1985, Missouri enacted strict pro-life legislation. By 1989, *Webster vs. Missouri* had wound its way to the Supreme Court. *Roe vs. Wade* was set to be overturned. The Bushies wanted no part of that. Consider the pro-*Roe* backlash from suburban women! *Roe*, as it turned out, wasn't overturned, but states could now enact restrictive policies.

Sam was immersed in voting patterns. Central to that was the rise of "ethno-politics." As the minority electorate rose and the white one fell, the Democrats now had a built-in advantage over their hapless Republican foes. To win, the GOP would have to earn at least 60 percent of the white vote. A despairing Francis noted how difficult that had become. It is hard to get whites to vote GOP in such numbers. He might have added that the abortion issue proved decisive. Suburban women, especially college-educated ones, indeed worried that *Roe* might be overthrown. So they flocked into the pro-choice camp.

What happened to the Reagan Democrats? Sam's analysis was spot on. The GOP's support for free trade, forever wars, and immigration, legal and illegal, annihilated the once-impregnable Nixon-Reagan coalition. Free trade deals sent jobs and industries overseas, costing the GOP states in the industrial Midwest. Immigration from Asia and Latin America knocked out the Anglo population in Southern California and the ethnic (Irish, Italian, Eastern European) vote in the New York City area. California and New York—gone!

With both the Persian Gulf War and the 2003 Iraq War, the Republicans alienated a generation of white-working class voters, the proles who would volunteer to fight—and die—in the Bush wars. In a late Nineties talk before a conservative gathering, Sam tried to explain this to his former allies. He praised Buchanan for scoring well in such Reagan Democrat strongholds as Macomb County, Michigan and Mahoning County, Ohio. By then, establishment conservatives had long rejected Sam Francis. They had also dismissed the once-admired Buchanan. America First fell on deaf ears and blind eyes.

Pat Buchanan and Sam Francis were now the voices of America First. And so, an eventful year, 1992. Historic for the GOP in that American demographics now moved against them. Francis was not the equal of Buchanan, but he was mentioned in the same breath as a presidential candidate. As important, Sam became more explicit than Buchanan. While the latter remained concerned with foreign affairs and ways to keep America out of forever wars, Francis increasingly became focused on race, culture, immigration, and the assaults on America's Eurocentric heritage.

Either way, Sam was now talked up as the intellectual driving force behind Buchanan's presidential campaigns. Along with Sobran, he was a pundit who stood with Buchanan during the latter's 1992 and 1996 campaigns and all the ferocious insults (racist, anti-Semite, "flirting with fascism," xenophobic, isolationist, protectionist) that were hurled against them. Pat Buchanan was the author of Buchananism. Sam Francis served as an intellectual double, plus an inspiration and friend while Buchanan was being savaged in the press. Barry Goldwater and Ronald Reagan had William F. Buckley, Jr. With Reagan, that tale ended in glory. Buchanan had Samuel T. Francis. The odds against a similar happy ending were substantially greater.

7.

A Populist Revolution?

AS 1992 YIELDED TO 1993, not all conservatives were unhappy to see George H.W. Bush gone. The right, as Buchanan observed, likes to be in opposition. Defending country club Republican Party administrations gets tiring. In opposition, the right could cut loose. For Sam Francis, that meant more than listening to Rush Limbaugh. The right needed to build an authentic community of Middle American Radicals.

Beginning in 1993, Ralph Reed's Christian Coalition (CC) took shape. When the Clinton Administration announced support for gays in the military, social conservatives were stunned. Membership in the CC rose exponentially. Reed made the rounds on cable and network television and radio talk shows. The CC drew members from across the country. Would-be presidential candidates appeared at CC conferences. Was the CC Sam Francis-style activism on display? Here was a national organization comprised of members paying modest sums growing to the point where politicians had to take notice.

The CC, however, did not last. The organization was hardly Buchananite. Its leadership were regular Republicans, nothing radical. The CC refused to take controversial stands on military intervention in Bosnia or Haiti. In 1996, Reed preferred Bob Dole over Buchanan in that year's GOP presidential primary contest. Hardly right-wing populism! The CC, Sam believed, could have made a difference. Reed was the successor to the Rev. Jerry Falwell and the Rev. Pat Robertson. When the latter was under assault from the liberal media, both William F. Buckley, Jr. and Norman Podhoretz sprang to Robertson's defense.

Why? Robertson commanded an army of millions sympathetic to the social policies that the intellectual right also supported. Such are the fruits of an effective populism. The CC, too, was hit on many fronts (anti-female, homophobic). What the CC couldn't do was address immigration and changing demographics. To take the Sam Francis position would now have the CC being slaughtered as racist, nativist, and xenophobic. That was a burden too great to bear. Religious conservatives supported the Bush wars in Iraq, Afghanistan, and Iraq again in 2003. That contributed also to their irrelevancy.

Sam Francis stayed loyal to the old crew. He continued to speak at John Randolph Society events. His column lit up the pages of both *Chronicles* and the *Washington Times*. As the nation continued to fall apart, Sam and his friends Fleming and Wilson went separate ways. Believing America to be doomed, Fleming and Wilson started the Southern League, eventually called the League of the South (LOS).

For years Fleming had traveled to Italy, where he became friends with members of that nation's successful *Lega Nord* (Northern League) party. Based in northern Italy, the party, under the charismatic leadership of Umberto Bossi, rolled up impressive numbers in that nation's northern provinces, so much so that it was able to join the right-of-center ruling coalition headed by the newspaper magnate-turned-politician, Silvio Berlusconi. Devolution seemed to be on the rise.

The *Lega Nord* opposed the European Union, illegal and legal immigration, and the transfer of tax dollars from the prosperous north to the welfare population in southern Italy. They also championed the regional cultures of that historic nation, a celebration that further attracted Fleming and Wilson.

In time, the *Lega Nord* would forsake regional politics and become a national force under the leadership of Matteo Salvini. The LOS was not a political party. It fielded no candidates in local elections. It offered a two-fisted support of the region's conservative heritage, celebrating the South's achievements in music, literature, political philosophy, and its orthodox Christianity. Rallies were held in support of the Confederate flag and a large monument to Nathan Bedford Forrest was constructed on private land in Nashville. Fleming and Wilson reached out to Sam without much success. The man was certainly concerned with cultural issues. Sooner or later, however, there would have to be political victories.

Sam would find other allies. The Council of Conservative Citizens (C of CC) was populist in nature, but also nationalistic rather than regionalist in outlook. It was derived from the old Citizens Council that sprang up in Mississippi during the civil rights era. In its day, the council was popular in the Magnolia State. A governor from the 1950s, John Bell Williams, saw some virtue in its existence. Instead of engaging in acts of violence against civil rights protestors, the average white Mississippian could attend a council meeting, express his opinion, and be among like-minded friends. The C of CC, due to those roots, was even more controversial than the LOS. The latter focused more on the South's Anglo-Celtic heritage than the race issue. Sam became a valued member of the C of CC, now believing that explicit language was needed to awaken the masses.

On a more conventional note, Buchanan, once 1992 ended, went back to his syndicated column and his nightly appearances on *Crossfire*. Pat and his sister Bay founded the before-mentioned American Cause. There were newsletters, pamphlets, and press releases, plus an annual conference. The 1993 get-together included Sam Francis as a guest speaker. He used it to inject more clarity into his ever-expanding populist message. American conservatism was over, defunct. What next? Conserve, hell! Might have been the war cry. It was time to dethrone the liberal/conservative elite. The talk was Sam's representative word for the early 1990s. Blunt as always, his first sentence hits the reader between the eyes and keeps him focused throughout: "The first thing we have to learn about fighting and winning a culture war is that we are not fighting to 'conserve' something, we are trying to overthrow something."

The old America, Sam added, wasn't entirely lost. Middle American Radicals still felt an allegiance to the country, 1950s version. There was a culture, a way of life, plus institutions and beliefs distinctly American and worth saving. However, Middle American Radicals had no allies in this fight:

> We must understand clearly and firmly that the dominant authorities in the United States—in the federal government and often in state and local government as well as the two major political parties, in big business, the major foundations, the media, the schools, the universities and the system of organized culture, including the arts and entertainment not only do nothing to conserve what most of us regard as our traditional way of life but actually seek its destruction or are indifferent to its survival.

And it gets worse:

> We still have a democratic political system in which opposition remains in principle legal, but we all know the difficulty encountered by those who try to use their civil liberties to challenge the dominant authorities. Genuine dissent from the egalitarian, feminist, homophile, multiculturalist, and socialist agendas of the dominant authorities is seldom permitted in the establishment media and often is outright punished, intimidated, or actually terrorized.

Either way, one can't quit. Francis called for the "organization of effective resistance" to the leftist agenda by honorable means:

> When I call for the overthrow of the dominant authorities that threaten our culture, I am not advocating illegal or undemocratic processes, but the war for our culture is a radical or even revolutionary conflict because it involves an almost total redistribution of power in American society—the displacement of the incumbent governing and cultural elites, the dismantlement of their apparatus of domination, the delegitimating of their political formulas and ideologies, and the radical decentralization of power and control of cultural norms from the hands of the present elite to those of the Americans who remain loyal to their traditional cultural and national identity.

Sam's rhetoric was changing. In the 1980s, he called for mass movements. That wasn't enough. Those movements must be out-and-out revolutionary. The liberal/conservative elite had to be overthrown, replaced by a righteous army of Middle American Radicals. Sam, as with most old-fashioned conservatives, had no use for democracy. It was the hand dealt to him and so he played it. Nor was he a monarchist as was the case of many a conservative nostalgic. He believed in a right-wing revolution, but as stated, only through peaceful means. Where to turn? It was time to find inspiration from the European Left. The new influence was Antonio Gramsci, an Italian Communist who languished in Mussolini's jails before perishing in 1931 at age 46.

Gramsci spent jail time writing his posthumously published *Notebooks*. A political revolution, Gramsci maintained, must be preceded by a cultural one. This was also a major theme of the Rockford Institute's *Chronicles*. Gramsci didn't accomplish much in his abbreviated life. He urged the creation of "workers committees" throughout his native Italy. Sam now advanced the idea of a shadow government-in-waiting. Nothing new here. This is what conservatives hoped to accomplish with the Heritage Foundation and the American Enterprise Institute (AEI). Once a Republican Party administration was in power, Heritage and AEI would supply the position papers and the personnel to carry out conservative goals: school choice, school vouchers, privatization of Social Security and Medicare, enterprise zones.

For Francis that was not enough. Privatizing Social Security was a gutsy idea Sam would support; however, it had no grassroots support. On the foreign policy front, AEI was instrumental in providing the ideologues responsible for pushing the failed occupations of Iraq and Afghanistan, the right's version of JFK's "the best and the brightest." Sam's populism was not about policy papers, although having an America First-style think tank couldn't hurt. It was about concerned citizens seizing power, first locally and then on to bigger game. Populists needed to embark on three major strategies.

First, expand and enlarge their numbers and adherents. Reject the D.C.-based conservative movement and the Republican Party. Money? Francis advised going outside the usual sources, namely large conservative foundations, for help. Is that possible? The Tea Party and the anti-Critical Race Theory (CRT) movements were bankrolled by wealthy individuals. In 1979, John Taunton, a Michigan physician, founded the Federation for Immigration Reform (FAIR), a longtime anti-legal immigration organization. Heritage, as noted, was funded by Colorado beer baron Joseph Coors. Roger Milliken, a South Carolina textile mill magnate, was long active in trade protection. Is that enough?

Second, raise Middle America consciousness. Sam worked tirelessly at this: editorials, columns, essays, books, speeches, conference talks, C-SPAN appearances. Francis also rejected a single-issue strategy. Wage culture war on all fronts. Yes, defend state flags, statues and monuments, traditional holidays (such as Columbus Day), public schools named for American heroes. Oppose a multicultural curriculum, promoting instead the heritage of the West from Homer to T.S. Eliot, plus the America of Washington and Jefferson, Paul Revere and Samuel Adams, Davy Crockett and Daniel Boone. The annual Right-to-Life March in Washington was grassroots politics in action but that was only a single issue.

A Populist Revolution?

Populists needed to create a seamless garment: fighting the culture war meant slaying the many-headed octopus destroying the traditional America:

> Long-standing issues of the populist right like abortion or new ones like homosexuality, school curricula and gun control cannot be seen or fought in isolation from issues that previously have not been issues at all such as trade, immigration, and an America First foreign policy. Activists should use all these issues to inform previously inactive citizens and groups of how they are all the victims of alien domination and of what they can do to resist it.

Third, a national movement. The triumphs that populists achieve in such minor frays as school board elections and city council races can be transported to the national level: State legislative races, congressional races, presidential primaries, a *national* movement—all with a populist base that maintains its original integrity. In a smaller European country with a populist third party up and running, that might be possible. In a continental-sized country like America? With no third party possible, a national movement would mean overthrowing local Republican Party chapters branch and root and replacing them with America Firsters. That represented an enormously difficult task. The GOP is well-stocked with lobbyists, money men, and PR experts determined that "this thing of ours" *never* succumbs to right-wing populism.

Thus, Sam Francis-style politics for the 1990s and beyond. A daunting mission. The decade started on a heady note. Take back our country! Take back our culture! How was that possible? American public culture derives mostly from New York and Hollywood. Both are wall-to-wall leftist. Television shows and movies mock traditional morality with great gusto. Both New York and Hollywood have no use for fly-over country. This includes the publishing world, sandwiched in left-wing Manhattan. Secondary schools, colleges and universities, graduate schools? The Ivies still set the pace. Liberalism is so dominant that FOX News, a "conservative" cable network, would be as anti-Donald Trump as CNN or MSNBC. Its mercurial owner Rupert Murdoch would fire the popular Tucker Carlson, who during the Trump era, began to voice Sam Francis-like opinions on immigration. School boards probably *are* the best place to start. And that can yield benefits.

Francis remained prophetic. The culture wars raged on. Future years would see the Tea Party movement organized to oppose Barack Obama's health care proposal. Later came parental opposition to the before-mentioned CRT. An idea hatched in academia, CRT posited that racism is ingrained in America. Angry parents disliked the rewriting of American history. More Sam Francis-style activism. In both cases, citizens and parents throughout the country didn't take cues from the Republican Party or what was left of the "conservative" movement. They acted by themselves.

In New York City, hard left Mayor Bill DeBlasio formed a commission to construct monuments to famous women in American history. Public input was permitted. The Gotham public overwhelmingly chose Elizabeth Seton, the Italian-born saint, as their favorite. The committee, chaired by the mayor's wife, rejected a Seton statue. The city's Italian-American community, up to 900,000 people strong, was enraged. They sprang into action, raising funds and constructing their own monument to their favorite saint.

When Confederate flags went down in South Carolina and Georgia, Southern patriots mounted a "Flags across Dixie" campaign, inspiring the battle cry, "when one Confederate flag goes down, three more go up!" When monuments to such icons as Robert E. Lee, Stonewall Jackson, Jefferson Davis, Jeb Stuart, and Nathan Bedford Forrest were removed, an organization, "Monuments Across Dixie" was formed.

The C of CC was involved in street theater, including pro-Confederate flag rallies and demonstrations to keep a mural of Robert E. Lee on display at a Richmond, Virginia park. On it went. In Colorado, the state's Italian-American community took action to keep its annual Columbus Day from being renamed. On the anniversary of the death of George Floyd, New Jersey tried doing away with its own Columbus Day. Garden State residents rose up and the holiday remained.

Sam Francis was a political animal. Culture first, then politics. Was that possible? The media doesn't mind a seminar in Charleston on the Vanderbilt Agrarians. When reactionary positions reach the realm of politics, another story. If a right-wing counterculture is a means to political success, then where's the success? And how with a Republican Party under pressure from FOX News?

The early Nineties did see movement on the populist front. There was Mary Cummins, the Queens County grandmother who single handedly fought condom distributions in the New York City public school system. In Colorado, a used car dealer garnered enough signatures for a statewide vote on an anti-gay rights proposition. Most spectacular was California's 1994 Proposition 187. Fed up with the inability of the federal government to secure the southern border, angry Californians petitioned for a referendum that would prohibit certain taxpayer-funded services to illegal aliens. In 1980, Southern California was mostly Anglo and Republican. 1990? An entirely different state.

Neither the Reaganites nor the Bushies did anything about immigration, legal or illegal. Southern California, once the heart and soul of conservative activism, was now multicultural and Democratic. Proposition 187 was Sam Francis-style politics in action: an authentic grassroots movement, ordinary citizens compiling the necessary signatures (and more) needed to put the question on the ballot. Pete Wilson, the state's Republican governor, eagerly jumped on board the anti-illegal train. However, the *Wall Street Journal's* editorial page, easily the nation's most militant proponent of open borders, came out against it. As did Jack Kemp and William Bennett, both of whom traveled to California to oppose the measure.

Proposition 187 passed easily, garnering more than 60 percent of the vote. Wilson was re-elected. Kemp's presidential aspirations were finished. No happy endings just yet! Liberals searched out an appeals court judge who, citing the 14th amendment, promptly ruled the referendum unconstitutional. California Republicans backtracked. In time, they deemed Proposition 187 to be a mistake. It alienated Latino voters, driving them further into the arms of the Democratic Party, making it impossible for the GOP to ever win the state. Latino leaders gloated that the referendum represented the last stand of Anglo California. Sam Francis's MARS foot soldiers were on the march. They were met with defeat, their hard work knee-capped by judicial tyranny, their cause betrayed by a Republican Party that wanted nothing to do with those rowdies. More bitterness, more frustration lay ahead.

8.

Purged

UNDER THE LEADERSHIP of Rep. Newt Gingrich (R–GA), the Republican Party in 1994 won control of the House of Representatives for the first time since 1952. They also took control of the U.S. Senate. Sam Francis was never impressed with Gingrich. He cared little for the "opportunity society" politics articulated by Gingrich and Jack Kemp. In an April 1995 *Chronicles* column, "Gnostic Newt," he ripped the Speaker for his New Age ways. Gingrich, Francis said, was a man with a "sophomoric mind." The Speaker was enthusiastic about an information-age style economy, declaring that it would break state control over what people read, watch, and digest. In the years hence, Francis's own career was kept alive by such technology, i.e., his column surviving in cyberspace. That wasn't enough. Sam preferred meat and potatoes politics: protective tariffs, safer neighborhoods, smaller government, more controls on immigration, and less meddling abroad. A laptop for every schoolkid wasn't on the list.

The 1995 freshman class billed itself as the most militant ever to hit the Capitol. Members called for term limits, some of them vowing to resign after only three terms. The Gingrich Congress approved a tax cut, a welfare reform bill, and a Defense of Marriage Act, all signed into law by President Clinton. On other issues, the freshmen had no impact: They opposed GATT, a global free trade agreement supported by both Clinton and Gingrich. They lost on legal immigration. Up to 77 Republican House members voted against a bill that would reduce legal immigration by a modest total. The freshmen opposed Clinton's air war over Yugoslavia and supported a government shutdown over budgetary disagreements. Gingrich became the model statesmen, supporting a taxpayer bailout of the Mexican government and working with the Clinton White House to reach a budget agreement, preventing a shutdown. A right-wing takeover of the party was averted.

On the stump, Pat Buchanan was kicking up dust. Popular in New Hampshire, the commentator was running second in national polls to Senator Bob Dole, the establishment favorite. Buchanan's populist themes hadn't changed. He opposed free trade and wars in Somalia and Yugoslavia, while supporting immigration reductions, a national holiday for George Washington, and promising to be the most pro-life president in American history.

Buchanan's rise focused attention on Sam Francis. Sam was being hailed as the mastermind of a Buchananite populism. Pundits surveyed the scene and wondered: Where was Buchanan's support in the conservative media? Joe Sobran sympathized mostly with Steve Forbes and his flat tax plans. William F. Buckley, Jr. and George Will could never be Buchananite. The same was true for Rush Limbaugh. Buchanan's populism was traced back to Sam Francis. The latter, along with Tom Fleming and M.E. Bradford, had hoped that Buchanan would quit a Republican Party that despised his America First platform.

In 1993, Buchanan should have declared himself a Third Party candidate for 1996, surfing on Perot's momentum while heading off the Texan at the pass. Fleming and Bradford visited Pat at his McLean home that year, making such a case. There wasn't any way the GOP would allow Pat to win the nomination. And if so, they'd sabotage him, 1964-style, in the general election. Declare now and build tremendous momentum for 1996. Buchanan demurred, explaining to his friends that he had to go back to *Crossfire* and his syndicated column to "put money in the bank."

Sam remained a Buchananite, writing favorable columns on his campaign while running down such rivals as Dole and Forbes. To Francis, Buchanan was running well for one reason: He was the only candidate with something to say, firmly addressing America's economic, cultural, and demographic path to national suicide. Sam was indeed becoming the voice of Buchananism. Fleming and Bradford were also correct: Buchanan, could never win the nomination. He could fight the world, but not win it.

As 1995 progressed, establishment conservatives trained their sights on Sam Francis. Point man apparently was John J. Miller, a Michigan native and vice president of Linda Chavez's Center for Equal Opportunity. Chavez was a native New Mexican popular in conservative circles. She was elevated to Director of Public Liaison during Ronald Reagan's second term. Her main duty was to steer Reagan's tax reform bill through the Democratic Congress. The bill passed and Chavez was on course to run for a 1986 Senate seat in Maryland. That race, in a Democratic year, fell short.

Chavez then formed her own think tank. When the immigration issue hit shore in the late 1980s, Chavez was with the establishment right's dominant immigrationist faction, assuring readers in *Commentary* that American culture faced no threats from these patriotic new arrivals. Impish as always, Sam had fun with Chavez's media visibility, referring to her in columns as the right's "Miss Chiquita Banana." Queen Victoria-style conservatives were not amused.

There was also Sam's increasing commentary on the race issue. Is Social Security reform the third rail of American politics? Yes, and the race issue is thermonuclear. When Sam published a newsletter, he covered familiar populist positions on trade, immigration, foreign policy, abortion, and gun control. He also announced that "Afro racists" would not escape scrutiny. By the mid-Nineties, the culture war against the South was in full blast. So were Francis's return volleys. Pundits across the spectrum, such as John Judis on the left and Tod Lindbergh on the right, admired Sam's prose style. Few wanted anything to do with Sam's explicitness. Conservatives feared a Francis-style conservatism would obliterate the GOP's minority outreach plans, alienate suburban voters, and send the movement and the party down to a Goldwater-like shellacking. On the respectable right, Sam Francis became a pariah figure.

Later, Miller confessed that he had long "wanted to run [Sam] out of the movement." As a member of the *Washington Times* editorial page, Francis, despite his utter contempt for Beltway conservatism, was now a star in that same constellation. Always on the lookout for allies, Sam found one in Jared Taylor. The latter was the author of *Paved with Good Intentions,* a history of affirmative action and the country's ongoing failure in race relations. Taylor had his book published by a reputable New York firm, Carroll and Graf, and reviewed in such respectable journals as *National Review*. That was the last time this attention would happen. Taylor, who was proficient in Japanese and a former resident of that island nation, first encountered Sam's writing in 1986 when the latter had a column published in the *San Francisco Chronicle*. "This is a liberal newspaper in a liberal town, but this man is one of us," Taylor recalled.

Taylor, a native of Kentucky, also lived in the D.C. area. The two became friends. Increasingly radical himself, Taylor, by the early Nineties, had formed an organization, American Renaissance, dedicated to a conservatism thoroughly Francis-like in its platform and blunt language. By 1994, Taylor felt he had enough momentum to hold an inaugural conference, one that could evolve into an annual event. Admitting that it was a risky financial undertaking, Taylor needed Francis to give a major address. Which he did. The talk was explicit, focusing on genetic differences and the survival of the West.

Sam showed a draft to Tom Fleming. The latter advised against delivering it. Sam had a key position at the *Washington Times*. Why risk it? Were the knives already out? Around this time Fleming had converted to Roman Catholicism and was concentrating on reviving a mordant Western Christendom. In a talk with this author, Fleming said Sam was essentially going to give his head on a platter to his legion of enemies. Fleming, as I recall, even made a gesture and an "here you go" similar to a waiter handing over a plate of food to a customer.

Francis did not take his friend's advice. The times, Sam felt, were opportune for such bold language. In 1994, The Free Press, a conservative-leaning New York firm, published *The Bell Curve*, co-authored by Charles Murray and Richard Herrnstein. Subtitled, "I.Q. in Contemporary America," the heavily researched volume explained that I.Q. levels do indeed determine economic success. By the 1990s, Murray was a celebrity on the right, mainly from the success of his 1985 best-seller, *Losing Ground*, a critique of the welfare state that gave momentum to welfare reform proposals on Capitol Hill.

By the *Bell Curve* publication, Herrnstein had died and Murray had to take the heat alone. *The Bell Curve* is a mild book. The authors worried that the facts would create an angry right-wing uprising, one where college-educated whites would join forces with working class voters, a combination that might destroy liberalism itself. The controversy came when the authors examined black and Hispanic I.Q. scores. That gave the Left its opening. Murray survived and went on to write other deeply researched best-selling books, including *Human Achievement,* which celebrates Western creativity in the arts and sciences, and *Falling Apart*, an examination of the continued destruction of white working-class America. Murray was learned and provocative, but not right wing.

Sam Francis was not so lucky. The American Renaissance conference was held, the speeches delivered. In his talk, Sam declared that there are indeed differences among the world's various peoples, cultures, and races. Sam was pro-Western, but in terms explicit: "The civilization that we as whites created in Europe and America could not have developed apart from the genetic endowments of the creating people, nor is there any reason to believe that the civilization can be successfully transmitted to a different people."

Sam's defenders pointed out that such talk was once commonplace. In the old *National Review*, circa 1957, such language would be as controversial as a mid-July weather report. After Sam's death, Chilton Williamson, Jr. defended the speech. Western superiority in the arts and science is merely an empirical observation, supported by thousands of years of achievement. Nothing new here. Pat Buchanan drew an analogy: "What Sam was saying was that when the Carthaginians perished, the Carthagian culture died with them. Had he said this of the Chinese and Chinese civilization, no one would have noted. But in these times, this was blasphemy."

The address, as Fleming feared, did not go unnoticed. Enter Dinesh D'Souza. The latter was a rising celebrity among establishment conservatives. An immigrant from India, he came to America in 1979 and attended Dartmouth University. There he joined Ben Hart (son of longtime *National Review* editor Jeffrey Hart), Jeff Kemp (son of Jack Kemp), and future FOX News star Laura Ingraham at *The Dartmouth Review*, an off-beat conservative campus paper that often made national news with its undergraduate humor. D'Souza later published a biography of the Rev. Jerry Falwell.

D'Souza worked in the second term Reagan White House and later became a fellow at AEI. *The End of Racism,* his 1995 book, was in the conservative mainstream of general optimism over the American prospect. D'Souza denounced radicalism on both the left and right. For the latter camp, Sam Francis was the target. D'Souza, as it turned out, was in attendance at the 1994 American Renaissance conference. His report was published a year later.

Sam Francis was back in the news. By this time he was already on probation. The anti-Francis faction at the *Times* had hoped to score earlier. They almost did.

In June 1995, the Southern Baptists, one of the largest religious organizations in America, held their annual convention. Southern Baptists, if united, can make a powerful voting bloc. This get-together was different. In the 1850s, Baptist leaders North and South were caught up in a serious debate over whether the Bible does in fact countenance slavery. As the debate raged on, neutral observers agreed that the Southern Baptist position—that it does— had the better end of the argument. A good fifteen decades later, the conventioneers decided to strike their earlier position from the books. They did so in public fashion, issuing tearful apologies. The subject was too hot to handle. Keep it a one-day story.

Sam, as was his habit, jumped into the fray. Slavery, according to the Bible, is not a sin. The peculiar institution to liberals is America's original sin. Segregation, likewise, is original sin number two. Sam rejected any admission of collective guilt. As he pointed out, *individuals* commit sins, not entire peoples. Further, the organization, according to Sam, was on the road to socialism. He started the column by quoting Oswald Spengler: "Christian theology is the grandmother of socialism." How so? Well, once one doctrine is demolished, the rest can go too:

> You can dismiss the New Testament passages about slaves obeying their masters as irrelevant today, but they happen to occur in the same places that enjoin other social responsibilities—such as children obeying their parents, wives respecting their husbands, and citizens obeying the law. If some passages are irrelevant, why should anyone pay attention to the others? Why not sign up with the feminists, the children's rights crusaders, and the Bolsheviks? So much for "Christian family values."

Sam Francis—prophetic again! In the Reagan Eighties, conservatives of all stripes were united on the definition of the family: father, mother, children. End of discussion. That conservatism has ended. In 2005, the then-conservative columnist David Brooks endorsed gay marriage. The floodgates opened. Kathleen Parker, a conservative who once opposed gay marriage, now as a columnist for the *Washington Post*, supported it. "Conservatives" now believe that the family *does not* have to be a father-mother-children unit. Same sex marriage is legal. Conservatives must accept it. A boy can grow up without a father. A young girl can grow up without a mother. Conservatism, 21st-century style, has rejected the Biblical injunction against homosexual behavior. They, too, have rejected the traditional family unit as the only one acceptable. They have indeed abandoned "Christian family values."

Francis noted that certain *Washington Times* staffers were upset by the column. Otherwise, it seemed just another day at the office. It wasn't. The next day, Sam was called into the office of Wesley Pruden, *Times* editor, and dismissed from his job. "Thunderstruck would not be my reaction," he wrote in a *Chronicles* column. Sam was out of work. He was also in financial straits. When he recovered from the shock, Sam explained this to Pruden, who along with firing Sam had also lectured him on his alleged insensitivity in writing a column that would offend the large black population in the D.C. area.

"I had not known that adults talked like this," Sam dryly observed. A distressed Francis softened Pruden. He gave Sam a reprieve. He could stay on at the *Times*. In addition to his syndicated column, his weekly editorial page contribution would rise from two to three. He took a cut in pay. Sam still had a meal ticket. He was also finished with the *Times*. "As I opened the door to leave, I was determined to get out of there," he vowed.

Francis would not hold his fire. The American Renaissance talk was given a year before the initial dismissal. Were Sam's superiors aware of his American Renaissance talk? The organization advertised the event. If the *Times* didn't know about the conference in 1994, they would learn soon enough. *The End of Racism*, as noted, was published in 1995. Excerpts were in the September 24, 1995 issue of the *Washington Post*. The article reproduced the Francis quote on biological differences. Portions of the D'Souza piece were inaccurate, so much so that the Free Press, according to Jared Taylor, had to destroy the entire first run print of the book, while the author hastily rewrote his version of the conference. A Third World immigrant trashed the descendant of early Americans.

Concerning Sam's fate, it didn't matter. Probation was over. Francis was again called into Pruden's office. This time, the dismissal was final. Sam had his readers. He had fans who had become followers. Some of them planned a demonstration protesting the firing outside of the newspaper's offices in northwest Washington. Sam immediately told the organizers to cease and desist. He also refused any telephone interviews. Francis, after all, had been determined to escape his old employer. He was out of a prized position—and weary of his time in the dock.

Francis remained defiant. He would not trim his sails in the slightest degree. He also remained convinced that his brand of conservatism would win out and that his enemies on the right would someday find themselves on that losing end:

> My column has actually gained newspapers since my defenestration at the *Times*. It's true I lost my job and my Washington outlet, and that's a blow, but it's far from death. In the coming years, the Beltway right may be amazed to discover how little it has to do with the direction in which the country is moving, and I plan to be there when it finds out that no one else is paying much attention to its precious "limits" on what you can and cannot say.

Always prophetic, Francis sensed there was a Donald Trump in America's future.

The Buchanan campaign rolled on, heading straight for caucus victories in Alaska and Louisiana, a second-place finish to Bob Dole in Iowa, and a world-shaking win in the New Hampshire primary. Were the 2020 Iowa caucuses rigged against Bernie Sanders? Did the same thing happen to Pat Buchanan in 1996? In the June 1996 number of *Chronicles*, James J. Conduit, Jr., a Buchanan supporter, discovered that point shaving had taken place in the Iowa contest. In Dubuque County, Buchanan scored 870 votes to 339 for Dole and 245 for Alan Keyes.

It didn't matter. The caucuses began at 7 p.m. At 6:56 p.m., Peter Jennings of ABC called the race for Dole. At 7:01 p.m., a minute after the caucus had opened, the Associated Press followed suit. The votes from Dubuque and the rest of the state were reported not to the Iowa Republican Party, but to an outfit called Voters News Service (VNS), located in New York. All of the major networks rely on VNS to make projections. With Dole projected as the winner, the boys at VNS shaved 113 votes from Buchanan's Dubuque total. Conduit noted that if similar vote shaving had taken place across Iowa, then outright victory was stolen from Pat Buchanan. The public will never know. The officials results of the February 12, 1996 Iowa caucuses have never been released.

Such vote fraud, if it occurred, had to happen. Bob Dole was a fragile front runner. A 32-year veteran of Capitol Hill, Dole, who was Gerald Ford's running mate in the 1976 loss to Jimmy Carter, had run unsuccessfully for president in both the 1980 and 1988 primaries. In 1996, Dole, who also served as Senate Majority Leader, was a front runner out of step with the populist insurgency of both Buchanan and the Republican freshmen. A loss to Buchanan in Iowa and New Hampshire would have finished off the Kansan. Who, then, would step in to stop Pitchfork Pat?

Buchanan's New Hampshire victory touched off a global panic, the forerunner to Donald Trump's 2016 campaign. For the next two weeks, Buchanan was the subject of one of the greatest outpourings of media hatred in American history. Charges of racism, xenophobia, nativism, and antisemitism, plus such milder broadsides as protectionist and isolationist, were slung Buchanan's way by the right/left media. The news was so overwhelming that Bay Buchanan, Pat's younger sister and campaign manager, kept newspaper stories away from the candidate, lest he lose his equilibrium. Unlike Trump, Buchanan did not have Twitter technology to snap back at his enemies.

After New Hampshire, Buchanan's next stop was Arizona. That state had never held a presidential primary so early in the season. To one-up other states, Arizona held early mail-in voting. Before the actual primary, tens of thousands of votes were already cast. Prior to the Alaska caucus, Steve Forbes, running a Perot-style billionaire's campaign, had jumped out to a lead in the polls, including a solid margin over Dole in Arizona. That mattered decisively.

On Arizona's primary day, Buchanan won the popular vote, repeating his New Hampshire victory. The nomination was within reach. And with it, the Sam Francis right-wing populist revolution. It was not to be. Buchanan's primary day victory could not overcome Forbes's early mail-in vote lead. Forbes was the victor. The next week, the South Carolina GOP machine came through for Dole. The Kansan won that state's pivotal primary. Buchanan's insurgency was over. Fleming, Bradford, and Francis were right about that third party run.

Sam Francis's dismissal from the *Times* was national news. Even *National Review*, a publication opposed to right-wing populism, defended him. In 1996, Sam remained at the center of controversy. After Buchanan's New Hampshire victory, Francis gave a talk at the annual Conservative Political Action Conference (CPAC) in Washington. When Buchanan was getting hammered in the media, the inevitable phone calls came to Sam's desk. The columnist told a *Wall Street Journal* reporter that Pat didn't share his beliefs on race. One has the feeling that this was rehearsed: Sam was willing to play the role of an extremist to Pat's moderation. That was the winter. The year was just beginning. Another attack was coming Sam's way.

In September, the John Randolph Club held its annual meeting at a hotel on the Jefferson Davis Highway in Arlington. The club had been formed as a joint association of Rockford Institute paleoconservatives and Mises Institute paleolibertarians. They shared social conservatism and opposition to American imperialism. This was to be the last meeting of the Rockford-Von Mises factions. On the campaign trail, Buchanan's mercantilism was more pronounced than ever. In the *Wall Street Journal*, Paul Gigot declared that Buchanan was the most articulate protectionist since the 1920s. Always the wit, Buchanan praised libertarians; he also joked that they paid too much attention to "dead Austrian economists."

That would mean Fredrich Hayek, author of *The Road to Serfdom,* the legendary 1944 tract against state planning. It also included Ludwig von Mises, the tireless critic of modern bureaucracies and the man that Lew Rockwell's Mises Institute was named for. Buchanan, once a free trader, was shocked by the demise of the Rust Belt. He now advocated tariffs on incoming goods to protect existing American industries while supporting tax and spending reductions to keep the economy rolling along. In short, the economics of Calvin Coolidge, a popular president.

Rockwell had long admired Buchanan, once calling him the "most important conservative in America." However, the quip about dead Austrian economists was the final straw. The Von Mises people had long disagreed with Buchanan on trade. As Rockwell wrote in a 1996 column, Murray Rothbard had consistently talked to Pat on the errors of his tariff policy. To no effect. At the Randolph meeting, Rockwell's talk was entitled, "Down With The Presidency." He approvingly quoted Randolph of Roanoke who once declared that his mission was to oppose the presidency of Thomas Jefferson lock, stock, and barrel. Rockwell's favorite president, he quipped, was William Henry Harrison. Why? Well, Tippecanoe served only one month before succumbing to pneumonia he caught during his own inauguration ceremony.

Rockwell's address was a prelude to the libertarian's major offensive. That came in a talk by Hans-Herman Hoppe, an economist who served with Rothbard on the faculty of the University of Nevada at Las Vegas. Hoppe took aim at Buchanan and Francis. In a talk comparing libertarianism to conservatism, Hoppe charged both men with being statists. Hoppe admitted that Francis-style politics properly attacked the Left's cultural war against American and Western history. It also opposed American-led New World Order conflicts around the globe. Plus, right-wing populism would eliminate the Departments of Education, Commerce, Energy, the Interior, plus the National Endowment for the Arts and the Equal Opportunity Commission. It was still statist.

Buchanan and Francis would return control of education to states and localities. That wasn't good enough. Education, Hoppe reminded listeners, was the domain of the family. The state should have nothing to do with educating other parents' children. Hoppe believed that any attempt at cultural turn around was impossible if the state were involved in the lives of individuals. The Buchanan-Francis worldview defended Social Security, Medicare, and unemployment subsidies. Trade protection, in the form of national import and export restrictions, was yet another example of expanding statism.

Hoppe was harsh. He claimed that the Buchananites detested "capitalism, laissez-faire, free markets and trade, wealth, elites and nobility," opting instead for a proletarian conservatism, which would merge social conservatism with socialist economics. In the Von Mises libertarian kiss-off to the Buchanan-Francis worldview, Hoppe played the ultimate card. In the published text, he maintained:

> Hence, [in the Buchanan-Francis platform] it is necessary to combine the economic policies of the left and the nationalism and culturalism of the right, to create [in Francis's words] "a new identity synthesizing both the economic interests and cultural-national loyalties of the proletarianized middle class in a separate and unified political movement." This doctrine is not so named, but there is a term for this type of conservatism: It is called social nationalism or national socialism.

Fleming, Francis, and Wilson were in the room, as was Paul Gottfried. While Hoppe spoke, everyone knew he was referring to Sam Francis. The latter was standing next to Fleming. As Hoppe continued, an angry Sam Francis paced back and forth, reaching into his cigarette case. Fleming followed Francis, trying to calm him down. The talk went on. During the question-and-answer period, attendees defended Buchanan, praising his genuine concern for America's beleaguered blue-collar workers. Hoppe's talk was later included in his 2005 collection, *Democracy: The God That Failed*. Francis, who died earlier in the year, would surely agree with much of its contents, including the critique of democracy itself. Hoppe presented a striking economic, moral, and cultural defense of libertarian thought.

Hoppe is a German immigrant who clearly prefers the Catholic monarchy of the Austro-Hungarian Empire—and its cultural inheritance—to the urban-industrial mass democracy welfare state that emerged triumphant after World Wars I and II. Central to his book was privatization, including the defense budget. Conservatives who once railed against big government made an exception for the Pentagon. Hoppe blew holes into that contradiction. The welfare/warfare state is Public Enemy Number One. Conservatives were guilty of supporting the latter.

As Hoppe continued, Wilson left the room. Your servant, attending his first Randolph meeting, didn't know what to make of Wilson's departure. I hung around. Fleming convinced Sam to leave the conference. The two joined Wilson in a lounge area where other attendees were recovering. Tom, Clyde, and Sam. Three of my mentors. Courteous as can be. Also at the table was a young Thomas E. Woods, Jr. We exchanged pleasantries. He talked about watching the second 1984 presidential debate between Ronald Reagan and Walter Mondale and being star-struck by the Gipper's poise, polish, and humor.

Tom Woods wasn't Reaganite anymore, but he reserved special praise for Reagan in his 2004 book, *The Politically Correct Guide to American History*. (In fact, Woods would make it to the *New York Times* best seller list with not one, but three provocative tomes. He outstripped us all.) Fleming tried to make light of the situation, singing "Hoppe *uber alles*" while re-filling his glass. Sam slumped back, puffing on a smoke, weary and dismayed, trying to crack a smile. First, Pruden. Now, Hoppe. What a year! Pundits are paid to be provocative, while backing up opinion with historical evidence. Which Sam, Fleming, Sobran, Wilson, and Woods were thoroughly capable of doing.

I had my books ready. Sam signed *Beautiful Losers*, Tom Fleming a pamphlet of a talk he gave in New York City on Columbus Day 1992, a good 500 years after the fact. A red-haired Sam Francis fan sat next to him. She admired Sam's writing greatly. The young lady also complained about walking through a mall in northern Virginia and "not seeing any white faces." This, I thought, was the ideal Sam Francis reader: an ordinary American girl, one who traced her ancestry to the British Isles, someone with roots in 18th century America, someone whose family had been living in northern Virginia for generations, whose ancestors had served in the military, who probably too had served in combat, whose family had owned land, an old stock American girl who now walks through a shopping mall without seeing any white faces.

This was the fall of 1996. The post-1965 immigrant surge of Asians and Latinos was beginning to overwhelm the Washington suburbs. Virginia was still red. A Jefferson Davis Highway ran through deep blue Arlington County. As Sam maintained in column after column, a red Virginia or a Jeff Davis Highway could not survive the immigration/demographic/leftist onslaught. Sam acknowledged his young fan. He didn't comment, familiar by now that his writings would attract fans eager to sit next to him. The next morning, the conference concluded. Tom Pauken, a Vietnam veteran and former Reagan Administration official and a future chairman of the Texas Republican Party, made the case for the Dole-Kemp ticket.

Sam spoke without notes. He declared that he left the Republican Party in 1993 after Kirk Fordice, then governor of Mississippi, pronounced the U.S. to be a Christian nation—and was immediately denounced by the GOP. Bill Kaufman asked Francis about the prospects for a successful populist movement from the left. In the 1992 campaign, former California governor Jerry Brown's run had shaken the Democratic Party establishment. Sam acknowledged the existence of a left populism, while maintaining that any successful populism would come from the right. Here Sam correctly saw the future. The Democratic Party coalition was confined to heavily populated cities and suburbs, an amalgamation of college-educated whites and minority groups. Rural America would become heavily Republican. As Sam could also have foreseen, the GOP could care less about such voters.

The purge of Sam Francis was only the latest in a pattern traced back to the 1960s. Antiwar conservatives, as Paul Gottfried has pointed out, usually got the shaft from establishment conservatives. That included Murray Rothbard and the John Birch Society, both of which had opposed the Vietnam War. The purges really took off in the 1980s and beyond. They picked up in 1981 when M.E. Bradford was denied a nomination as chairman of the National Endowment for the Humanities (NEH). Gottfried had lost a graduate professorship at American University in Washington, D.C. after Norman Podhoretz declared that Gottfried wasn't hawkish enough on Israel.

Sobran's antiwar position, which started with the Persian Gulf War and continued into the Clinton years, led to so much tension at *NR* that the columnist simply resigned. Scott McConnell got sacked as editorial page editor of the *New York Post* over the issues of Puerto Rican statehood and immigration. McConnell had pushed the *Post* into the restrictionist camp. Prominent New York politicians of Puerto Rican heritage complained to the *Post's* management, which promptly buckled. Buchanan kept his journalism career. The media onslaught, which establishment conservatives piled on, took care of his political one.

Was Francis's career saved by the Internet, an electronic phenomenon just coming into its own? Friends thought so. That madhouse is home to millions of crackpot views. Sam's writings, as no one can deny, were thorough and scholarly. A man of print, Francis nonetheless hailed the Internet as an outlet capable to making an end run around the media elite. Sam found a benefactor. Sylvia Crutchfield, a Virginia woman of means, came to the rescue. The latter, according to Gottfried, constantly worked in the background, raising funds for numerous right-wing causes, including those to help Sam make up for his lost earnings at the *Times*.

Francis no longer commuted from Maryland to northwest Washington. His trip to the workspace in Alexandria was longer. "A writer must write!" the bombastic Hollywood mogul Samuel Goldwyn once lectured his charges. Sam didn't need any hectoring. He was a writer on a mission. His columns, essays, speeches, correspondence, and manuscripts all went forward. Sam had plenty of fight in him. He no longer had an outlet in respectable conservatism. Was that a blessing or a curse? An end or a beginning? Fortified by friends and well-wishers, he soldiered on.

9.

Conservative Wars

"SAM WAS ON A ROLL," so claimed Louis March, recalling Francis's life after the *Washington Times*. Sam was saved by the Internet and the generosity of Ms. Crutchfield. At its peak, Sam's column ran in 50 publications but declined steadily. He still had the *Chronicles* column, plus those in *Middle American News, American Renaissance,* and *Southern Partisan*. On the web, a different story. Peter Brimelow's popular VDARE.com site carried the column, as did *The Unz Review*, founded by Ron Unz, a one-time pro-immigration activist who had performed a 180-degree turn on that issue. Through it all, Sam never complained over his fate. He was glad to leave the *Washington Times*. Once dismissed, he stayed as busy as before, combining various writing projects with regular speaking engagements. To the relief of his friends, he began to lose weight, while also kicking the nicotine habit.

The 2000 election was one of the closest in American history. On the eve of the tally, George W. Bush held a slim lead in the polls. Shockingly, he lost the popular vote to Al Gore by 500,000 tallies, while winning Florida by all of 535 votes, thus salvaging the presidency. The nation's division, at last, was laid bare. Sam Francis had his own take. Race was the issue driving the wheel. George W. Bush, Sam declared, owed his 2000 victory to white voters. Francis approvingly quoted Steve Sailer: "The reason George W. Bush struggled so much to eke out a 271-267 win in the Electoral College is not that he got crushed in the minority vote. No, it's because he commanded only a measly 54 percent of the white vote."

The odds of Americans facing up to their fate remained slim. The enormity of the issue is too great. A media onslaught would take care of any racial consciousness-building. Sam carried on. His Southern homeland remained under siege: numerous columns were devoted to the Confederate battle flag fight in South Carolina. Pro-flag organizations were driving forces supporting the old banner. Rallies in 2000 saw up to 10,000 people rallying for the flag at demonstrations in Columbia and Montgomery. The South Carolina GOP, under heavy pressure from the national party, caved in, removing the flag from the capitol dome.

The Georgia legislature followed suit, dropping the 1956 state flag and its battle flag insert for a bland, blue banner that was rejected by the electorate. The cultural cleansing ended temporarily when Mississippi voters in 2001 voted to keep the flag as part of the 1894 banner. Sam Francis-style politics was at work. Activists obtained more than the 100,000 signatures needed for a referendum vote. From there, the "yea" vote won by a 3-1 margin. As important, neither the Mississippi nor the national GOP had anything to do with the referendum.

Why all the commotion over a flag? Especially in states that supply a large percentage of troops in an all-volunteer U.S. armed service? "Who would have thought 100 years ago that the Confederate flag would be the most important issue in the United States?" Fleming asked the crowd at an LOS Montgomery rally. "Nobody would have thought it." The United States was becoming undone. Liberals and conservatives were blaming the flag of a long-vanquished nation and symbol of a region. In 1976, the flag meant *The Dukes of Hazzard* and Lynyrd Skynyrd. By 2000, the nation was engulfed in a culture war. The flag's appearance now meant that the South was behaving in a subversive manner.

Sam had denounced "secessionist fantasies" from the right. He knew, however, that attacks on the Confederate flag were just the beginning. It was the nation's entire Western heritage that the Left was after. That included Thomas Jefferson. In the late 1990s, the Left scrambled to deflect the raging controversy over the Bill Clinton-Monica Lewinsky scandal. The Jefferson-Sally Hemmings hoax, concocted during the 1804 election by a British journalist, was drummed up again, mostly to prove that Clinton's behavior wasn't *that* bad, but also to discredit Jefferson's standing as an inspiration for anti-big government movements.

Sam was only too happy to blast back, noting in a *New American* essay that the source of the libel was John T. Callender, a partisan hack with a drinking problem that led to a premature death by drowning. No testing has ever proved Jefferson to be the father. Jefferson, Francis reminded his readers, was a beloved figure in his day, a man who followed Washington's example of voluntarily giving up power and gratefully returning to his plantation. As with Washington, the Sage of Monticello was a wonder of the age. Men just don't *give up* power. Jefferson did, and in doing so, gave hope to a tired world. As with the Confederate flag, Sam, by defending the now-reviled Jefferson, was rowing upstream.

Sam Francis at first had some hope for the Bush administration. Neoconservatives had rallied behind the candidacy of John McCain, whose hawkish credentials were never in doubt. Any hope for Bush was short-lived. After being sworn in, Bush moved quickly to champion amnesty for illegal aliens, a move that Sam denounced as a Munich-like appeasement, not to mention a blatant betrayal of Bush's hapless working-class constituency. Bush wanted amnesty. He wanted it quickly. Get it over with. On September 11, 2001, the Republican-controlled House conducted a "yea" voice vote to grant amnesty to anywhere from 7 to 11 million illegals. That day, every single living body on Capitol Hill had to clear out. Literally. They ran for their lives. As the House was voting for amnesty, 19 terrorists—all of whom, as documented, had entered the country legally—were blowing up both the World Trade Center and the Pentagon.

Now thoroughly part of the antiwar right, Francis had plenty of company in opposing the 2002 war against Iraq. In 1991, an antiwar coalition on the right took shape in the form of an opposition to the

Persian Gulf War. The coalition of Tom Fleming's traditionalists and Murray Rothbard's libertarians had developed an articulate full head of steam.

The John Randolph Club, of which Sam was a charter member, came out not only against the Gulf War, but other post-Cold War conflicts, including the 1992 invasion of Somalia, initially designed to assist starving people in that nation's civil war that had morphed into an adventure in nation-building by the Clinton Administration. That opposition extended to the abortive invasion of Haiti in 1993, a NATO bombing war in Bosnia in 1995 over a Balkan civil war and, finally, the 1999 repeat, this time in Serbia over that same Yugoslavian civil war. The antiwar right found its voice in Buchanan's 1999 history, *A Republic, Not an Empire*, a plea for the U.S. to stay out of wars that have no bearing on its national security.

For the Iraq War, the opposition culminated in *Neo-Conned!* a comprehensive two-volume set, published in 2006. The collection included essays by an eclectic group of free thinkers: Francis, Fleming, Rockwell, Sobran, Bill Kauffman, Allen Carlson, and Wendell Berry, the prolific poet, essayist, novelist, and short story writer, a man who opposed the Vietnam War and who had long been a favorite of liberal environmentalists. Berry, a registered Democrat, was also pro-life on abortion. Shunned by the Left, he found plenty of admirers on the antiwar right.

Neo-Conned! was published by IHS Press, a Norfolk, Virginia-based conservative pro-Catholic house. The Iraq War, opponents believed, violated every possible just war concept as articulated throughout the centuries by Catholic dogma. A just war is a matter of self-defense. When attacked, fight back. War, however, must only be made by armed men against other armed men. Iraq, a country with the Gross National Product (GNP) the size of Kentucky, could do no damage to the United States.

In the wake of 9/11, the Bush Administration was able to convince a frightened public that Saddam Hussein, the longtime Iraqi dictator, was constructing Weapons of Mass Destruction (WMD) to be used against the United States. Which never was the case. A large portion of the public even believed that Saddam was responsible for the 9/11 attack. That, too, made the Bushies case easier to make.

By then, another round of the Conservative Wars was underway. By March 2003, a real war had started. Baghdad, Iraq's capital, had fallen to coalition troops. Saddam had been captured. Bush declared a "mission accomplished." The former Air Force reservist celebrated a May 1, 2003, victory landing on the *U.S.S. Abraham Lincoln*. The war on terrorism was real: trillions spent, thousands of American lives maimed or lost. It was also a phony war. There was no draft, no declaration of war, no sacrifice on the home front. Americans consumed foodstuffs and pumped gasoline into their automobiles. The occupations of both Iraq and Afghanistan proved difficult. Both wars were becoming unpopular. Establishment Conservatives sensed this.

Buckley assigned David Frum, a Canadian-born pundit, to pen the before-mentioned *National Review* essay, "Unpatriotic Conservatives." According to Richard Brookhiser, Buckley pressured Frum to be as harsh as possible on the dissenters. Frum zeroed in on a cast of apostates, including Buchanan, Robert Novak, Lew Rockwell, Tom Fleming, Sam Francis, Justin Raimondo, and Scott McConnell. Frum was familiar with paleoconservatism. He devoted a chapter on their worldview in his 1994 book, *Dead Right*. He noted their opposition to mass immigration and previous American wars, while detecting a whiff of antisemitism from Kevin McDonald, author of *The Cult of Dissent* and another antiwar rightist. (McDonald had long contended that major Jewish groups had lobbied for the 1965 immigration bill, one that paleos had long lamented.)

Except for Buchanan, the war's critics, Frum acknowledged, were unknown to the public. *National Review*, as the conscience of the right, had to take a stand. The opposition, Frum claimed, had made common cause with left-wing and Islamist movements in both Europe and America, while "explicitly [yearning] for the victory of their nation's enemies." Concluded Frum: "War is a great clarifier. It forces people to take sides. The paleoconservatives have chosen — and the rest of us must choose too. In a time of danger, they have turned their backs on their country. Now we turn our backs on them."

Sam Francis used his space in *Neo-Conned!* to respond to the unpatriotic charge and to articulate the entire paleoconservative opposition to the conflict. Unpatriotic? Not a chance. Down on the government? That, since 1932, has been the story of an authentic conservatism:

> The paleos in general are disaffected not from the country itself but from the determination of the U.S. government to wage unnecessary wars that either border on the unjust or actually go well over the line of injustice, wars that are unprovoked and are not clearly in the interests of the nation, whether just or unjust, and wars that, even if victorious, may lead to so many entanglements, complications, injustices, and costs (human, economic, diplomatic, technological) that they are better avoided, regardless of their moral character. What most paleos have written about the Iraq war has been along these lines—lines that are perfectly consistent with and indeed reflect a serious patriotism, as opposed to the kind of sophomoric chauvinism that demands blind obedience to whatever wars the government launches.

A *book* could be written on Sam's talent for prophecy. The wars in Iraq and Afghanistan cost the taxpayer up to $8 trillion dollars. The costs included a weakening economy resulting in the sub-prime mortgage crisis, the 2008 stock market crash, the subsequent decline of the Western economies, the rise of a totalitarian China, the election of Barack Obama, two leftists justices for the Supreme Court, and the triumph of same-sex marriage that the right once hotly opposed. For establishment conservatives, it was all worth it.

War for what? When the United States withdrew from Afghanistan in 2021, its military were chased out by the same Taliban terrorist squads the U.S. had initially defeated.

Meanwhile Bush, in 2004, squeaked through with a 51-48 percent re-election win over the Democratic Party nominee, Senator John Kerry (D—MASS). Sam held no brief for Bush. He seemed bored with the election. As the vote approached, he told readers that if they were also uninterested, they could read a good book. In this case, it was Chilton Williamson, Jr.'s *The Conservative Bookshelf*. Williamson chose 50 works ranging from The Bible to *The Sun Also Rises*. Sam's 1997 collection, *Revolution from the Middle* was included, as were works by Fleming, Wilson, Buchanan, Weaver, Sobran, Kirk, Burnham, T.S. Eliot, Ernest Hemingway, William Faulkner, G.K. Chesterton, C.S. Lewis, Edmund Burke, Henry Adams, and everyone's favorite, Flannery O'Connor. Williamson's mission was to define conservatism once and for all, declaring it to be "man's willingness to discern for himself, and to accept from God, a fundamental, practical, just, human, and unchangeable plan for man—*and to stick with it*."

Williamson praised Sam's tireless efforts in *Revolution from the Middle* to rally Middle American Radicals. Prospects remained bleak, but that was hardly the fault of a single pundit. Fight on into the darkness and "it is at least conceivable that the present situation will need to deteriorate, rather than improve, before popular opposition to it takes form at last."

Francis was unimpressed with Bush's re-election. He ridiculed the president for winning only a "pathetic" 58 percent of the white vote nationwide, while running against a liberal senator from Massachusetts. The theme of the campaign boiled down to values. Again, Sam was critical. What values? Indeed, there was one. In 2003, the U.S. Supreme Court by a 5-4 vote, struck down a Texas anti-sodomy statue. Liberals had found the successor to *Roe vs. Wade*. Abortion was once illegal in all 50 states. With the victory in *Texas vs. Lawrence*, so, too would same-sex marriage be legalized throughout the land.

Conservatives and Republicans tossed up a half-hearted opposition. President Bush reiterated his support for heterosexual marriage only. Karl Rove, Bush's campaign manager, cooked up a pro-marriage government initiative. House and Senate Republicans proposed a constitutional amendment. Such an amendment, Francis claimed, was unnecessary. Congress has the power to control the Supreme Court's docket: what cases they can hear, which ones are off-limits. All Republicans had to do was to use their majority to prevent the court from hearing challenges to 1996's Defense of Marriage Act (DOMA). That alone would prevent the courts from imposing same-sex marriage on the 50 states. Republicans were no more serious about defining marriage as solely between a man and a woman than they were in overturning *Roe vs. Wade*.

Conservatives, over the decades, had mellowed on this issue, from opposing "homosexual marriage" to "gay marriage" to simply, "same-sex marriage" to finally, caving in and endorsing the court's *Obergfell* decision. When David Brooks, in 2004, endorsed gay marriage, the D.C. conservative community was in shock: I thought this guy was on our side! Conservatives quickly fell in line. In the 1980s, with Ronald Reagan riding high, conservatives ridiculed the entire gay rights agenda. No chance! Approaching the 1988 election, Vice President George H.W. Bush claimed in his journal that voters "would never go along with the homosexual marriage" agenda of the Democratic Party. He was right. But not for long. Bill Clinton, who defeated Bush in 1992, supported gays in the military. That was a turning point. The pro-gay onslaught from the media (i.e., the television show, "Ellen," the movie, *Brokeback Mountain*) worked. Public opinion shifted. Bush 41 was no conservative. He was, however, a Republican. This native of Connecticut, a resident of Texas, attended a lesbian marriage ceremony at his Kennebunkport, Maine summer residence. The Bush team made sure the media knew all about it.

Sam Francis used the term, "homosexual marriage." Unlike Bush, he stuck with it. ("These people are *not* gay!" 1980s-style Moral Majority-types would exclaim.) In 2004, Republicans were only too happy to exploit the controversy. Numerous states placed referendums on the November ballot. Voters throughout the Midwest and the South voted overwhelmingly to define marriage as between a man and a woman. It worked for Bush 43. However, the GOP, as Sam Francis would have told anyone who cared to listen, had no desire to follow-up and take meaningful action. Even with solid majorities in both the House and Senate, they would skip that simple vote to control the court's docket.

10.

Explicit

SAM FRANCIS PLAYED a major role in putting paleoconservatism on the map. The term was conceived by Paul Gottfried as a rejoinder to a dominant neoconservatism. Paleos were Old Right conservatives. They had no use for the Buckleyites or the neoconservatives. Francis was always the realist. As the 1996 political season ended with Bill Clinton's easy re-election victory, Francis declared paleoconservatism to be finished. It had kicked up some dust in the late Eighties and early Nineties. Buchanan's presidential campaigns gave the term heightened publicity. Still, the man fell short. Elected GOP officials firmly opposed his campaigns. Buchanan's fourth place showing as the Reform Party candidate in the 2000 race only confirmed Sam's prediction.

With Buchanan spent as a political force and with the job at the *Times* lost, Sam entered the wilderness phase of his career. A man with nothing to lose? Sam's writing became more explicit than ever. His associates were light years away from the conventional conservatives at the Heritage Foundation. Sam wanted it this way. Paleoconservatism had run out of steam. Francis went looking for new allies.

"Explicit" is the title of this chapter. That describes the tone of Sam's later work. The 1994 speech marked a turning point. Sam was going to be explicit on the race issue. What of it? Francis was banished to the fringes, anyway. Might as well make the most of it. The goal now was to raise white unity. Some of this was Sam being his usual impish self. Since Reagan's 1984 re-election, conservatives and Republicans have engaged in a lengthy minority outreach program, culminating with George W. Bush's support for illegal alien amnesty and the latter's proficiency in Spanish. Sam liked to be contrary. Minority voters? Fine. Also go pell-mell after white working-class and middle-class voters. Maximize white enthusiasm and turnout. He felt this was a necessity not just for the survival of the Republican Party but for said people.

Francis was not always so explicit. During his time at Heritage, the new third rail never entered his work. Apart from the King essay, *Beautiful Losers* rarely touches on the issue. That volume was more concerned with the managerial class and how they gain and keep power. In time, however, the American crisis, to Sam, came down to this taboo. After the 2000 election, he was the first to dramatize the sharp red state/blue state divide. He believed differences were not merely cultural: Madonna America *vs.* Merle Haggard U.S.A. No. That election and those before and after were about the racial divide. James Burnham mourned the passing of the great European empires. He fretted over European nations losing their dominant role in the world. Sam, on the other hand, saw the next logical step from loss of empire— loss of nations, with the conquerors being conquered by their former subjects.

The shift to racialism would now define his career. If this biography is ever reviewed, the identification of Sam Francis as a "racist" will overshadow everything else he thought and wrote about. The word is a constant in everyday political discourse, used to intimidate conservatives and Republicans straight out of their socks. In time, Sam would have to confront it.

A 1999 essay, "The Origins of Racism," did just that. The subtitle described it as a "useless word." Its origins are recent. The Oxford English Dictionary traced its debut to Laurence Dennis, an antiwar, anti-New Deal journalist, who used it in his 1936 book, *The Coming American Fascism*. With further research, Sam claimed the honor instead belonged to one Magnus Hirschfield, a German medical scientist and prolific author. Hirschfield died in 1935. In 1938 his book *Racism*, written in 1933 and 1934, was published posthumously. Hirschfield was a player in revolutionary times. His specialty was "sexology."

Hirschfield seemed determined to break down traditional bourgeois values while spreading the gospel of sexual liberation, including acceptance of homosexuality. Along the way, Hirschfield encountered roadblocks. His fellow Europeans, indeed, his fellow world-citizens, held fast to traditional ways, including old-fashioned tribalism. A German Jew, Hirschfield even criticized his co-religionists for promoting Zionism, claiming it poisoned relations between Jews and Arabs. He championed a "Pan Humanism" for a tired world. Humans, he contended, needed to give up on the bonds of family, neighborhood, language, and nation and instead "seek kinship with humanity at large."

A tall order. Hirschfield became frustrated, blaming "xenophobia, xenophobia, xenophobia" for this failure. For him, Joseph Stalin's Soviet Union represented the ideal community. Here, at last, the problem of race and nationalism had been overcome. A true humanity was possible.

Is "racism" a useless word? What Sam meant was that the slur is the domain of the Left. It has only a polemical usage. Since "racism" represents Leftist terminology, the hard right would have to develop new strategies to confront it. Was that possible? Its usage is potent. No man was more prophetic about America's decline than Sam Francis. Here, he may have fallen short. Did Sam underestimate the power of the word? Is it more powerful than even Sam Francis realized? Is it not a word that can destroy a man? Can it not bring down entire nations? And how could the right ever overcome the racism smear hurled against them?

Francis would have to address the charges now leveled against him. He denied being a racist, even though he believed there are differences between races and cultures. Sam was now the star at Council of Conservative Citizens and American Renaissance confabs. It kept him in the news. Both organizations were considered well beyond the pale, even though Trent Lott, Richard Gephardt, and George Wallace, Jr. had attended C of CC gatherings. Lott even wrote a column, one that focused on economics, for a C of CC newspaper. In fact, Lott inadvertently put the council on the radar.

In 2002, the GOP regained the control of the U.S. Senate. Lott was in line to become majority leader. It was soon unearthed that the man, at a testimonial for Strom Thurmond, said that the country would be in better shape if the former had won his 1948 States Rights third party run for the White House. As with numerous Southern Democrats, Thurmond had long foresworn his earlier support for segregation. The nascent social media got wind of the event, and Lott, unable to make light of the toast (it wasn't uncommon to praise Thurmond), resigned his position.

There's no such thing as bad publicity. After Lott's clumsy resignation, news of his involvement in the C of CC was revealed and interest in the hitherto unknown organization soared. The media connected the dots back to its most famous member. In a column, Sam defended his friends and himself: "The C of CC is pro-white. So am I."

Sam Francis believed that the United States regime had become antiwhite. America's entry into World War II was the turning point. It was, he wrote, a war that became a social revolution. Most obvious was immigration and the makeover of the American population. The nation's Anglo beginnings succumbed to influxes from northern, central, southern, and eastern Europe, plus Japan and China. During the 1950s, trickles of immigration came in from the Caribbean and the Middle East. The U.S. and U.K. were both under pressure from Asian countries to let more of their people into the Anglo-Saxon nations. In 1965, the dam broke. Congress approved an immigration bill desired by the recently martyred president. The National Origins Quota was lifted and now immigration came 85 percent from Asia and Latin America. The bill, as Senator Sam Ervin (D—NC) pointed out, *did* discriminate— against potential European immigrants.

Before that, more revolution. During the 1950s and '60s, conservatives regularly criticized the *Brown vs. Board of Education* Supreme Court decision. They did so on both legal and cultural grounds. The Buckleyites briefly sided with the white South. By the Seventies, that was over. Conservatives since have spent decades trying to overcome the stigma of that opposition. When the 50th anniversary of *Brown* rolled around in 2004, the only dissent came from Francis, Buchanan, and Thomas Sowell, with the latter lamenting the demise of healthy public schools in the black community. Sam's column cited an essay by the historian Raymond Wolters that appeared in *Occidental Quarterly*. Wolters, author of the book *The Burden of Brown*, made his own case against the ruling:

> The rationale of the Court was spurious. Historical research has established that the framers and ratifiers of the Fourteenth Amendment did not intend to outlaw school segregation. It is hardly conceivable that the Congress that submitted the Fourteenth Amendment intended to destroy the states' rights to maintain segregated schools when that very same Congress provided a system of segregated schools in the District of Columbia. Moreover, several of the ratifying states continued to operate segregated schools without perceiving that they were in violation of the amendment.

> The evidence with respect to original intent is so clear that it discouraged even legal historian Alfred Kelly, who was working on *Brown* for the National Association for the Advancement of Colored People (NAACP). Kelly recalled that, "The problem we faced was not the historian's discovery of the truth. The problem instead was the formulation of an adequate gloss to convince the Court that we had something of a historical case."

The *Brown* decision relied heavily on sociological findings. Segregation allegedly gave young black children feelings of inferiority. Wolters, according to Francis, also dissected that argument:

> The psychological experiment involved all of 16 children in South Carolina. But the psychologist who conducted it, Kenneth Clark, never disclosed that the same tests given to "hundreds of black children who attended segregated schools in Arkansas and unsegregated schools in Massachusetts" showed the opposite result. If the test "was a valid means of indicating what sort of schooling enhanced black self-respect," writes Professor Wolters, "the data tended to favor segregated schools."

Sam's apocalyptic forebodings reached new heights. Here, at last, was America the irretrievable, the collapse of once-vibrant, safe, and industrious American cities, verily, the end of civilization. Establishment conservatives just don't write like this:

> The constitutional and scientific flaws of the decision pale before what it has done to American schools, cities, and the people who created them. By cramming through a legally groundless ruling that authorized the federal engineering of American society, *Brown* alienated Southern whites for at least a generation, wrecked public education and helped revolutionize both cities and suburbs.
>
> Today, schools once entirely white because of segregation laws are entirely black because of *Brown*. The white middle class exodus has meant the domination of cities by a black underclass,

the crooks and demagogues it puts in office and the financial and social devastation of American urban life.

In 1964, Barry Goldwater, Ronald Reagan, William F. Buckley, Jr., and George H.W. Bush (then running for a U.S. Senate seat in Texas) all opposed federal civil rights legislation. Buckley and Bush later repented. For Francis, federal civil rights legislation was never about achieving a color-blind constitution. It represented just another power grab. In 1971, the Nixon Administration enacted its affirmative action "Philadelphia plan" that imposed quotas on construction job hirings. That same year, the U.S. Supreme Court ruled in its *Briggs* vs. *Duke Power Company* decision that the 1964 civil rights bill could indeed be used to enact affirmative action programs.

The 1971 passing away of the Abraham Lincoln and George Washington holidays, respectively February 12 and February 22, was not antiwhite in nature. America was not yet that kind of country. Efforts to revive the holiday have come in vain. While running for president in 1996, Buchanan pledged to restore Washington's birthday as a national holiday. In time, GOP lawmakers filed legislation for such a commemoration. Sam wrote a column praising the virtues of the first president and those of having a holiday in Washington's name. In an age of multiculturalism, there was never any chance of passage. Few lawmakers signed on.

Antiwhite activity extended to American history. Francis had already weighed in on the consequences of the King holiday. The post-1987 "hey, ho, Western civ has got to go" nation saw campaigns against Confederate flags, the shamrock being displayed in Boston housing projects, efforts to have homosexuals march in St. Patrick's Day parades, and an assault on Columbus Day. The culture war went from the streets to the textbooks. There are also the sins of omission: the 1993 National History Standards failed to list not just Booker T. Washington, but also Paul Revere, Patrick Henry, Robert E. Lee, Thomas Edison, and Jonas Salk.

There was also, as Sam predicted, a war not only against things Southern: Confederate flags, statues, monuments, public schools, and highways, but against men once revered: public schools for Washington (New Orleans, San Francisco), Lincoln (Berkeley and San Francisco), Jefferson (Chicago, San Francisco), Andrew Jackson (Philadelphia) all renamed. The same with monuments in the riot-torn America of June 2020: Washington (Washington, D.C.), Columbus (Minneapolis, Chicago, Baltimore), Ulysses S. Grant (San Francisco), Jefferson (Portland, Oregon), and for the once-beloved Lee and Jackson in Richmond and Charlottesville.

The day after the Lee statue was assaulted, a mob called for the same to a similar equestrian statue to Washington at Richmond's state capitol grounds. Governor Ralph Northam did nothing to stop the attack on Lee, while swearing never to touch the Washington monument. Another mob attempted to tear down the Andrew Jackson monument across the street from the White House. That failed as the federal government and not the District of Columbia has jurisdiction over that property. The left plays for keeps. The National Guard had to protect the Lincoln Memorial from another angry mob.

Such acts of vandalism took place after Sam's death. He, thankfully, did not live to see the triumph of barbarism in the United States.

But he did prophesy it all.

Sam Francis confronted barbarism head-on. There was the column on the Washington birthday holiday bill. There were numerous columns on the South Carolina Confederate flag controversy, the 1956 Georgia state flag flare-up, the perennial attacks on Christopher Columbus, plus a long feature in the *New American* defending the legacy of Thomas Jefferson and destroying the Jefferson-Sally Hemmings hoax.

Establishment conservatives pride themselves in conducting color-blind politics. It is liberals who play the illiberal race card. Yet Reagan, to his critics, practiced the "dog whistle" strategy. As election time approaches, round up those white voters. Reagan's "I believe in states' rights," comment at the 1980 Neshoba County, Mississippi state fair was clearly ad-libbed. Reagan's talk focused on Jimmy Carter's high-inflation economy. His broadside against the welfare queen from Chicago ventured into Goldwater country.

Most explicit was George H.W. Bush's famed Willie Horton ad during the 1988 presidential campaign. Behind in the polls, the Bush team debated using such an ad, criticizing the Democratic nominee, Massachusetts Governor Michael Dukakis, for paroling Horton, a black man, who upon his release committed more heinous crimes. Bush signed off on the plan. The ad worked. The election ended with a Bush victory. James A. Baker III, Bush's friend and campaign manager, palmed off the entire idea on Lee Atwater, a top Bush operative. Baker came from Houston money and had a degree from Princeton. Atwater, a native of Columbia, South Carolina, played the blues guitar and spoke with an accent. A smart move.

Conservatives, as noted, were appalled by Francis's language. To them, Sam's blunt appeals conjured up the worst excesses of the 1950s and '60s-style conservatism. Those same conservatives and Republicans made brazen appeals to white voters. Why can't I do it? Sam probably wondered. There was a practical side to all this. The GOP needed white voters to win elections. They needed them to vote in large numbers. It was an angry and fearful white working-class and middle-class vote that gave Richard Nixon and Ronald Reagan their landslide wins, not to mention the GOP's 1994 takeover of the House and Senate. Why allow that working-class and middle-class constituency to disappear into an irrelevancy?

On the right, Francis stood alone. Conservatives routinely scorn liberals for race obsession. The left, to say the least, could care less. They play identity politics with a vengeance, convinced that it holds the key to past, present, and future victories. Is it so? The Democratic Party presidential nominees have won the popular vote in seven of the past eight presidential campaigns, from 1992 to 2020. They march forward: accusations of police brutality, white privilege, white fragility, support for affirmative action and quotas, continued mass immigration, legal and illegal, plus amnesty for millions of illegals already in the country.

Republicans, meanwhile, are convinced that liberals are on the road to political suicide. Asian and Latino voters will grow tired of bossy white liberals now running the party. Suburbanites will oppose Critical Race Theory for singling out their children for abuse. Plus, immigrants have "family values," making them natural Republicans. Will it happen? Republicans believe so. (The 2024 election results suggest it is possible.) Which is another reason why they didn't bother with Sam's warnings.

Francis had allies. Buchanan and Sobran remained friends. Jared Taylor and Peter Brimelow were happy to stand with him. Brimelow defended Sam from personal attacks. He pointed out that Sam had purchased a home in Seabrook, which happens to have black-majority residents. Sam, as Brimelow approvingly observed, lived in peace with his longtime black neighbors, none of whom, we can guess, knew that their neighbor—an unassuming middle-aged man, wearing a pullover sweater, hair falling over the forehead, quietly chain-smoking and wise-cracking along—was the most controversial political columnist in America.

This individual had no quarrel with the GOP's long-running minority outreach efforts. He saluted black achievement in American history and believed the rising generation should be aware of such contributions. He wrote a column praising the integrity of J.C. Watts, the former University of Oklahoma football star turned congressman from that state, when the latter got into a feud with Newt Gingrich. He especially admired Star Parker, the California housewife and conservative activist who supported the Buchanan candidacies and later the Trump presidency. Francis believed that above all the GOP should protect and mobilize the white working-class and middle-class vote.

The Nixon-Reagan landslide America is gone, but enough of it remains to put the GOP over the top. Protecting non-elite whites would mean keeping American manufacturing jobs at home while preventing working-class youth from coming home in a box at Dover Air Force base. It would also mean preserving the America that voted for Nixon and Reagan with a total cut-off of all immigration legal and illegal and the deportation of all aliens, including those who entered the country legally but overstayed their visas. It conjured up an old Texas saying: Don't forget the one who "brung you to the dance."

Explicitness was a matter of confronting ideology with ideology. In a summer 1998 talk before a packed house at the Soldiers and Sailors Club in New York City, Sam was his usual self. The left, he claimed, was anti-white, anti-Western, anti-Christian, anti-male, anti-heterosexual. Meet fire with fire. A true right, then, should be pro-white, pro-Western, pro-Christian, pro-male, pro-heterosexual. More than the survival of a single nation was at stake. An entire civilization, the greatest the world has seen, was on the line. Sam Francis would vigorously explain and defend that world with all the scholarly skills at his disposal.

11.

A Pep Talk for Western Man

EVER SINCE 1987 and the triumph of multiculturalism, conservatives have been thrown on the defensive over "the West." Conservatives feel forced to make the liberal case. The West stands for individual freedom. It expands rights to women, minorities, immigrants, gays, and lesbians. Establishment Conservatives, along with the left, believe the West is universal. Its value system applies to all men in all nations for all time. It transcends the old boundaries of land, culture, religion, ethnicity, and race. The triumph of the secular West is inevitable. The light it shines is too brilliant to ever be resisted.

In 1996, American Renaissance held a forum on the West. Jared Taylor made a positive case, citing democratic government, respect for women, freedom of speech, the rule of law, and concern for animals and the environment. Western culture, he added, gives "priorities to considerations of fairness over the exercise of pure power." Taylor wondered if such tolerance could survive in a multicultural society.

Francis didn't disagree with Taylor's assessment. He simply felt his defense was too liberal. The West, Taylor seemed to be saying, is not as bad as it is cracked up to be. That wasn't enough. Stronger medicine was needed. His response was, "The Roots of the White Man." It took off from there. Through the years Francis wrote several signature essays that captured his evolving worldview. I would list "Message From MARS," "America First," "Winning the Culture Wars," "Nationalism, Old and New," and "Pat Buchanan:

From Household to Nation." "The Roots of the White Man" stands with those. The essay, over 10,000 words, is a bid to go straight to the heart of the matter: where Western man sprang from, his history, characteristics, and achievements explained and, just as keenly, his shortcomings too, lest they prove fatal.

Conservatives write about "Western man." Sam opted for "white." From there, he went full throttle. Western man equals white man equals Aryan man. This surely is what Jared Taylor was talking about when he wrote that Sam exceeded boundaries that even made his friends nervous. Sam, too, acknowledged that "Aryan man" is a non-starter, due to its implication with European fascism. Still, Sam maintained the definition was biologically correct. And so, he proceeded.

The essay was a milestone in Sam's career. It defined his later writings. On a less dramatic level, it was just one of the many such statements in an age of multiculturalism. Western man had distinctive traits. He accepted a Cosmic Order of work, war, art, science, and self-government. He didn't live in a defensive mode: no, he traveled by land, sea, and air. He put an emphasis on sports and war, maritime and space exploration. Western man originated in the Russian steppes. It gets cold up there. Wanderlust existed in the heart of the species. Western man proceeded south to today's India, hence the beginnings of an Indo-European civilization. From there, it was north to Europe, where Western man found a permanent home. Wanderlust—and empire—followed, reaching an early zenith in the days of Alexander the Great and Julius Caesar.

The modern world took off in 1492 with Columbus's great voyage, followed by those of Da Gama, Magellan, and Captain John Cook. Hence, not only the Age of Discovery, but of the "white flood," European peoples streaming into North and South America, southern Africa, Australia, and New Zealand. There were consequences. These land spaces were not uninhabited. Western man's encounters with non-European peoples gave him an awareness he previously did not have. Western man, according to Francis, became aware of his pigmentation, eye color, hair color, facial features. From the beginning, Western man has always sought to separate himself from different peoples.

Western man, to Francis, was hardly privileged: throughout the centuries he was brave, bold, courageous, daring, inventive, passionate for life, and industrious, capable of creating stable communities. Western man accepted a tragic fate. He would not hide from his enemies. Magic would not save him. No deliverance from the gods was forthcoming. He would fight, even when defeat was pre-ordained. Western man would come home with his shield or as a dead man laying upon it. He accepted the dangerous life. He preferred a short life full of heroic deeds to a long one spent in servitude.

Life, however, wasn't always so dramatic. Western man, from the time of Plato onward, sought to construct an ideal political entity. Sometimes, he went too far, seeking for a utopia in a fallen world— with bloody results (see the 20th century). Western man, to Sam, was good at striking a balance. He believed in self-government, the creation of councils and parliaments. Society functioned harmoniously with separate and well-defined classes: monarchs, aristocrats, landowners, warriors, priests, merchants, and laborers with dignity. Status was earned. A nobleman inherited his position, but he had better strive to keep it. Richard Weaver once lauded the Old South for its "aristocracy of achievement" (Washington, Jefferson, Madison, Marshall, Lee, Randolph, and the Carter families). Sam, I believe, would agree. On self-rule, Western man was adamant. He would rebel if self-government were denied him.

Balance also meant harmony of the world of the individual with that of family, church, and community. *Individualism* was a hallmark of Western man, but he did not live for himself only. Individualism meant a man willing to walk alone. To Francis, it also meant working alone in a room writing, composing, sculpturing, painting, experimenting, and inventing. The results are evident enough. Achievements in astronomy, biology, chemistry, earth science, physics, mathematics, medicine, technology, and music are mostly Western. Those in art, literature, and philosophy are overwhelmingly so.

Sam Francis accepted modernity. His focus was on Western man and his restlessness, a man always on the move, on the offensive, creating, creating. Away from technology there was the more pleasing turn to art. A Sam Francis critic, Jason Rose, claimed Sam lacked a literary element to his work. Not so. Sam was well-read on all aspects of Western achievement: history, literature, philosophy, criticism, theology. Western man distinguished himself in the world of art: painting, sculpture, music, literature. Sam focused on sculpture. Oriental art featured blank faces. Western art was different. It celebrated man in his fullness: expressions of joy, anguish, doubt, and resolve.

For literature, Sam turned to Shakespeare. *Pace* Rose, Sam absorbed Shakespeare among countless other writers. He had a Ph.D. in English history. With Shakespeare, the full complexity of human experience bursts open: tragedy, comedy, histories. Larger than life characters, tragic madmen, tragic non-actors, doomed lovers, plus a happy ending or two. Western man confronted life. He knew evil existed in the hearts of men, but some glory was possible, too.

What good came from Western man and his thousands-year-old odyssey? Sam picked up on Taylor's earlier theme of chivalry. Western man honoured the fairer gender. Women were not merely slaves as in so many cultures. Western man believed in Divine Love. Women were to be loved. They were to be revered. They were life-long companions. As opposed to other cultures, no European woman could be in a harem.

Civilized behavior, too, extended to animals. Western man was granted Biblical dominion over beasts—and he practiced it. He revered creatures. Horses were valued as indispensable partners in both war and peace. So, too, was the hybrid, the ever-dependable mule. This reverence extended particularly to canines. "Man's best friend," yes. An indispensable one, too. Dogs were needed for the hunt so marksmen might track down the mammals needed to supply foodstuffs. As Grady McWhiney observed, the old America had a saying: "Do what you want with my wife but leave my dog alone." A joke, of course, still life without horses and canines was unthinkable—and unbearable. Treat them right.

Western man, Sam concluded, had a thousands-year-old legacy worth saving—and enhancing. Self-government, inventiveness in arts and sciences, a class structure producing harmony and self-worth, respect for women and animals. However, the defining quality is *courage*. Sam quoted Davy Crockett: "Be sure you are right, then go ahead." Western man was willing to fight and die under great odds, knowing that in defeat he planted seeds of victory. ("Remember the Alamo!")

The essay is provocative and meant to be that way. By using such words as "white man" and "Aryan," Sam was setting himself up like a bowling pin. After the *Washington Times* firing, he could take it. One riveting paragraph gets to the heart of the matter:

> Aryan dynamism is not confined to military conquest and geographical exploration. It is also clear in the Faustian demand to understand nature. Just as Aryan warrior nomads overturned whatever cities and peoples stood in their path, so Aryan scholars and scientists have conquered nature and its mysteries, discarding myths, religions, and superstitions when they presented obstacles to their knowledge, and systematizing their discoveries and thought according to the Cosmic Order.
>
> Alexander the Great's solution of the Gordian Knot by simply slashing it to pieces with his sword is no less a racial trait of Aryans than the scientific achievements of Plato and Aristotle, Galileo and Newton, and hundreds of other scientists who were heirs of the ancient Aryans and who slashed through obscurantism and mythologies with their minds.

And the world historical consequences:

> Their descendants have cured diseases, shrunk distances, raised cities out of jungles and deserts, constructed technologies that replace and transcend human strength, restored lost languages, recovered forgotten histories, stared into the hearts of distant galaxies, and reached into the recesses of the atom. No other people has ever dreamed of these achievements, and insofar as other peoples have ever known such things were possible, it is because they have learned about them from European Man.

Yes, you wished Sam hadn't used "Aryan man." More fuel for his detractors. The essay was part-history, part-*agent provocateur*, part pep talk. Western man must prevail. Still, he is human. And that came with real flaws.

Sam's criticism had a familiar ring to it. There was Western man's Faustian nature: the belief that he could have "pure and limitless" space in this world. Such vanity was the outgrowth of Alexander the Great's and Julius Caesar's conquests, not to mention the overseas empires in the wake of Columbus. That gave birth to something even more foolhardy: the cockeyed belief that Western values are universal. Western man, Sam observed, got so caught up in his achievements that he believed they could be transported to the entire planet. Sound familiar?

Sam and his allies relentlessly attacked the global "democracy promotion" crusade sought by both parties. Democracy, for better or worse, was a European invention. Do non-European peoples want it? During the presidency of George W. Bush, the answer was a resounding "yes." Skeptics on both the right and left wondered out loud if democracy could be transported so easily to the Middle East. Bush believed that lust for freedom burned in the hearts of men. Opponents observed that countries in that region—and throughout the world—had no experience in living under liberal democracy. Religion matters, too. The rise of Islam especially got in the way of secular democracy.

There are deadly consequences to empire-building. Western man used his superior technological advantage to conquer the planet. There were financial benefits. Most important, the European empires allowed missionaries to spread the Gospel to formerly heathen lands. There also was the boomerang effect: the United States, for instance, fights and loses in Cuba, Vietnam, and Afghanistan. It now must accept Cuban, Vietnamese and Afghan refugees, some of whom commit heinous crimes against American citizens. Britain gives up on India. It too must allow endless streams of Indian immigrants into the island nation. France retreats from Algeria. On their heels are North African refugees. This is liberalism in action. Liberal democracy as in immigration from non-Western nations.

Sam Francis described this phenomenon as the "back door route." Ancient Rome was a precedent. The Eternal City was flooded with immigrants, not only from northern Europe but from Africa and Asia. All roads led to Rome. And that proved to be Rome's undoing. Sam quoted the Roman poet, Juvenal: "The Orontes [the main river of ancient Syria] empties its garbage into the Tiber." Did America copy Rome?

> The Roman political and military success was not the end of the story, because the very success of Roman imperialism made inevitable the eventual inundation of their people and culture by those whom they had conquered. The importation of masses of alien slaves into Italy and their eventual emancipation, and massive immigration of foreigners from the Asiatic parts of the empire meant that the Indo-European racial and cultural base of Rome would eventually die.

Samuel T. Francis and Revolution from the Middle

The backdoor route consumed Rome. This, too, was the story of the post-1945 West. Since then, the reel, as Burnham foresaw, has been spinning backward. The European empires, under pressure from the United States and the United Nations, folded shop. Their former subjects raced after them. The Global South sought to flood the Global North. Not just the old colonial powers of London, Paris, Berlin, Amsterdam, and Brussels, or America's empire of liberty, but also such countries as Canada and Sweden. Others—Italy, Austria, Switzerland, Denmark, not to mention the former captive nations of Eastern Europe—were holding the line.

Western man believed he was invincible. He could conquer the planet not only physically but ideologically. His way of life, secular democracy, he believed, will yet prove irresistible. Sam decried the "missionary zeal" of Western man. His strength was creating and sustaining self-government. His art captured man in all his complexities. His desire to change and reform alien societies was an undoing. The alien world's multi-millions would exact their revenge.

Sam's most striking example of Western greatness comes back to the idea of courage. It is not unique to Western man. However, it has defined his existence for centuries. Sam used American models. Let's take the scene of a great event: the Alamo— Crockett, Jim Bowie, William Travis, and their band of 200 men knew they could not defeat Santa Ana's superior numbers of 4,000. Travis drew that line in the sand. Death—or surrender. To Sam, that was Western man at his finest. He knew he would lose. He knew, also, that he must fight. This was an Anglo-Saxon-Celtic culture at its zenith. Western man, Sam maintained, needed to recover a conceptual view of his heritage. In "Roots of the White Man," he did just that. It all comes back to courage. No worthy life can be without it.

In his final years, the race issue dominated Sam's writings. A flyer for the 1994 American Renaissance conference was defensive: Why is race so all-encompassing? It is as if Francis and Taylor wished it weren't so. Aren't there more pressing concerns, such as dismantling the welfare state and giving Americans local control over their own affairs? Did Taylor and Francis fear the race issue would consume and swallow up the United States? Or did they fear an intimidated GOP could not stand up to the race-obsessed Leftist onslaught?

Francis believed the issue was a global phenomenon, agreeing with Sir Roger Scruton, the British conservative who feared a "West vs. the Rest" scenario in which the thoroughly outnumbered Western nations stood no chance of survival. Yes and no. China is not engaged in a West vs. the Rest contest. It seeks benevolent rule over the planet. The race issue consumes certain nations.

Pat Buchanan believed that the new century would revolve around a world where race, religion, and ethnicity would determine the affairs of men. That might be closer to the mark. The 1979 Iranian revolution put Islam back on the political map, just as Hillarie Belloc had predicted. The troubles in Ireland have long been over religion. India, with its Hindu-Muslim tensions, is similar on a significantly larger scale. Factions on the right envy "ethno-states." They do exist: China (90 percent ethnic Han), Poland (98 percent ethnic Polish), Russia (80 percent ethnic Russian), not to mention Japan. In its thousand-years history, only two non-ethnic Japanese have ever been granted citizenship.

Sam Francis agreed with the Buchanan thesis. Still, he zeroed in on the "r" word. He subscribed to *The Camp of the Saints* scenario, where the Third World multi-millions invade and conquer a supine Europe. He remained steadfast in believing American public culture was antiwhite. Francis was stuck holding a taboo subject. He wanted to raise conscious unity among white Americans. Being on the outs helped. No respectable conservative can do that lest they be banished into darkness. Francis rejected America as a "universal" nation. Throughout its history, America has had periods of both mass immigration and of moratoriums. Up until 1965, however, immigration was confined to European peoples. The nation's leaders, in both parties, wanted it that way.

America's republican tradition, Francis believed, was not universal. It sprang from an Anglo-Saxon-Celtic culture. America, to Sam Francis, was a republic. It was an extension of the West, a nation informed by the examples of Rome and Athens, plus the Swiss federation. No multiculturalism. Was America, post-1987, part of the West? Education in the old America centered on preparing the gentleman for leadership in both times of war and peace. Knowledge of Greek and Latin were necessary to gain college admission. These were the founding languages of Western civilization. America was part and parcel of that world. In the 1917-1987 America, the Western civ requirement survived. Immigration, changing demographics, and multiculturalism is routing the Western tradition. With cries of white male, white privilege, and white fragility, liberals are *very* explicit. If a conservative makes a similar defense of the West— well, meet the fate of our subject.

Consciousness raising, to Sam, was a matter of survival. But how could it be successful? The left controlled the nation's institutions: universities, public and private schools, endowments, the entertainment industry, publishing houses, journalism, law schools, and in a final blow, corporate America. The drumbeat of American history as racist is all-consuming. Pushback comes from the Internet, but conservative writers and voices go up against constant intimidation. Opponents do not have a political party they can rally behind. That proved decisive.

Sam's pessimism continued to reach new heights. All looked to be lost: a nation, a history, a people, a culture, redeeming myths. Even the physical safety of ordinary Americans was at risk once they stepped out of the house.

12.

Anarcho-Tyranny: America Surrendered

SAM FRANCIS WAS NOT a single-issue columnist. Right to the end he wrote about the Iraq War, the state of conservatism, government tyranny, and attacks on Western and American history. He remained pro-life, pro-traditional marriage, pro-Second Amendment, anti-free trade. The culture war against American history was always present. The engine driving the wheel was mass immigration, legal and illegal, from non-Western nations. Sam's writings on immigration were so intense that they were collected in a volume with a most characteristic title: *America Extinguished: Mass Immigration and the Disintegration of American Culture.*

Immigration has been an on-again, off-again issue in American history. Francis focused mostly on the 1965 Immigration Bill and its consequences. The bill reflected America's new standing as the leader of the Free World. How could a democratic nation refuse immigrants from non-Western countries? Isn't that "racist"? Sam's view was that America's entry into World War II was a social revolution.

After World War I, Asian diplomats pressured both the U.K. and the U.S. to allow for Asian immigration into those two nations. London and Washington both said "no." World War II was different. This time they caved, fearing the newly independent nations of Asia and Africa and the resentful countries of Latin America would turn to Moscow if the Anglo-Saxon nations did not liberalize their immigration laws. The 1950s saw a trickle of immigration from the Caribbean and the Middle East. It also saw the Eisenhower

Administration's "Operation Wetback," a military-style maneuver that pushed some one million illegals out of the Southwest. At that time efforts to boost legal immigration failed.

The Kennedy Administration was the turning point. John F. Kennedy, the Irish-American son of a Boston millionaire, held a longtime grudge against the 1924 law that placed a limitation on immigration from Europe. Kennedy was determined to undo that law while adding slots for immigrants from Asia and Latin America. The move went nowhere on Kennedy's brief watch. The Senate subcommittee on immigration was chaired by Richard Russell (D—GA) who believed the U.S. should remain an Anglo-Saxon nation. After Kennedy's assassination in 1963, expanded immigration was given new life. In 1964, Kennedy's team published *A Nation of Immigrants*, a collection of the late president's speeches on the subject.

In 1965, legislation that eliminated the National Origins quota was approved. The floor manager for the bill was Senator Edward Kennedy (D—MASS). Kennedy, his brother Robert, also a U.S. senator, plus such solons as Daniel Inouye (D—HI) and Philip Hart (D—MI) all claimed the bill would not change the population makeup of the United States. Senatorial opponents such as Strom Thurmond (R—SC) and Sam Ervin (D—NC) turned the argument around, claiming the new bill would in fact discriminate against potential European immigrants. Thurmond and Ervin agreed with Russell. America derives from an Anglo-Saxon culture. The U.S. should remain a predominantly Anglo-Saxon nation.

Were the proponents serious in their claim that the new immigration rules would not change the population make up? Then why have Liberals been delighted by the transformation of America from a Western to a multicultural nation? Since the early nineties, the Democrats have won the popular vote in seven of the past eight elections. Changing demographics were key to that sea change.

That wasn't all. By the early-1970s, illegal immigration became a problem. Mexico's population was exploding while America's borders remained open. The illegal immigration issue sporadically rose up, to be defeated by "nation of immigrants" ideology. For conservatives, 1980 was their year of deliverance. But something far more significant took place that year. Ted Kennedy ran a losing race to upend Jimmy Carter as the Democrats' presidential nominee. Kennedy exacted his revenge. Repeating his 1965 performance, he shepherded legislation through the Senate that would dramatically increase legal immigration through family reunification: an immigrant could bring in with them not just a spouse and children but dozens of relatives: grandparents, aunts, uncles, cousins, nephews.

During the Eighties, immigration, both legal and illegal, skyrocketed. Nineteen seventies southern California was Anglo and Republican. By 1990 it was multicultural and Democratic.

In *Southern Partisan* Fleming published articles opposing legal immigration. In 1986, Francis brought out *Exporting Revolution*, a study of smuggling operations, an essay that focused more on infiltration than on demographic change. Three years later, Fleming, now editor of *Chronicles*, published the October 1989 "Nation of Immigrants" number that called for immigration restriction, jump-starting the right's ongoing war over this nation-breaking issue.

Francis shared Fleming's hawkish views. The cover artwork for *America Extinguished* is instructive. For *Revolution from the Middle*, the cover featured a single candle burning in the darkness. A light flickered. Hope existed. For *America Extinguished*, American culture, as with hope itself, had been snuffed out. Another candle, this one red, white, and blue, melting onto death.

In 1996 Chilton Williamson, Jr., Sam's brother-in-arms at *Chronicles*, published *The Immigration Mystique: America's False Conscience*, a history outlining the nation's opposition to mass immigration from the 18th century to present times. The first immigration law limited citizenship to free white people. From 1880 onward public pressure resulted in various reforms: restrictions based on health and literacy tests, the Asian Exclusion Act of 1908, and the immigration cut-offs of 1921 and 1924. All were examples of Sam Francis-style politics.

The 1921 and 1924 moratorium bills were the bounty of an active citizenry. Republican voters, heavily based in the Midwest, New England, and the Northeast, worried now about losing Anglo-Saxon America in the wake of Ellis Island immigration. True Americanism was at stake. In 1920, Warren Harding promised a return to "normalcy" under an America First platform. He won a landslide victory among a war-weary public. In 1921, legal immigration was reduced from 800,000 per annum to 300,000. Harding's successor Calvin Coolidge advanced Harding's restriction agenda. In 1924, Coolidge used blunt language, promising a wholesale moratorium. That year Coolidge was elected in a 38-state landslide. By then, the 1924 bill had been approved, further cementing another GOP victory.

Sam Francis did not dwell as much on immigration history as Williamson. His ambivalence about Ellis Island was a result of his admiration for Donald Warren's Middle America Radicals. They came from Sam's native Southland, but also from the put-upon Northeast and Midwest ethnic neighborhoods, now suffering crime, busing orders, and de-industrialization. The Milwaukee Serb Hall's audience of Serbian and Polish-Americans who eagerly welcomed George Wallace were valued foot soldiers.

All of this was consistent with the coalition-building of the Nixon years, as envisioned by Kevin Phillips of the Bronx and Patrick J. Buchanan of Washington, D.C. The Archie Bunker/Jerry Falwell coalition. Sam admired Italian-American culture and such pols as Rep. Tom Tancredo (R—CO), Rep. Lou Barletta (R—PA), and radio host Bob Grant. It was the 1965 immigration bill that brought down Euro-America and with it empowered hatred for the West and America's founding people.

For Sam Francis, no surrender. He countered a *reconquista* of the Southwest with the Anglo version: a *reconquest* by Americans. Reconquer the Southwest for the American side, not just by sealing the border but by deporting those tens of millions of illegals. Give up the Southern secessionist fantasies, Sam told Fleming and Wilson.

Get your country back. There were precedents: the 1921 and 1924 immigration bills and the Eisenhower Administration's Operation Wetback.

Here was the goal. And in time, the wars, both polemical and political. Finally, decades of frustration, defeat, and despair. When *Chronicles* 1989 "Nation of Immigrants" number was released, reaction was furious. Norman Podhoretz declared, "I know the enemy when I see one." According to Fleming, Rockford lost millions in grant monies.

In 1989, establishment conservatives saw no danger from mass immigration. Influenced by Pat Buchanan's culture war stemwinder at the 1992 Republican National Convention, Scott McConnell of the *New York Post* soon became a convert to the restrictionist camp. The biggest influence the embattled *Chronicles* crowd had was *National Review's* brief conversion. In 1965 that journal, then at its peak opposition to the federal regime, expressed concern about that year's immigration bill, asking if it would lead to more legal immigration. In 1968, Buckley defended Enoch Powell's legendary anti-immigration "Rivers of Blood" speech given in Birmingham, England. During the 1970s, *NR* occasionally addressed the illegal alien crisis, but the Cold War remained the pressing concern.

Buckley, in a "What's Next" essay, mentioned large-scale immigration and its potential for dividing the country. In 1992, after Buchanan's challenge to George H.W. Bush fell short, *NR*, under its new editor, John O'Sullivan, took the plunge. In its June 18, 1992 number, O'Sullivan published a long essay by Peter Brimelow, making a moral, economic, and cultural argument against mass immigration. Here, too, artwork mattered. The cover featured an angry Miss Liberty holding up a huge stop sign.

National Review prides itself as the pacesetter for conservative thought in America. Here, *NR* wasn't successful in gaining converts. *Commentary* and *American Spectator* continued their pro-immigration stance. *Human Events* criticized illegal entries, but not the legal variety. The *Wall Street Journal* editorial page would never consider running an op-ed against legal immigration. For years it ran an annual Fourth of July editorial calling for a "let there be open borders" amendment to the Constitution. The *Journal* also ripped the GOP for its "nativist" stance.

On the web, Peter Brimelow's *VDARE.com,* named for Virginia Dare, the first English child born in the New World, ran Sam's columns and became the daily gathering site for anti-immigration activists. Concerning *NR*, Francis and Fleming were pleasantly surprised. The nation's most important conservative journal of opinion had taken a Sam Francis-style stand on immigration. O'Sullivan did not shy from the cultural consequences. *NR* defended the United States not as a multicultural nation but as a Western one, derived from its Anglo-Saxon founding: its core culture, language, and legal systems. Articles asked if such immigrant-heavy neighborhoods as New York City's Washington Heights were recognizably American at all.

The *NR-Chronicles* coalition couldn't last. In 1996, Buchanan made another serious run for the GOP presidential nomination. Francis was on board, but *NR*—and Buckley himself—could not make the plunge. Neither could Joe Sobran or Rush Limbaugh. *NR* defended Buchanan against charges of antisemitism. It also advised Bob Dole, the eventual nominee, to take hard right positions the Kansan had no desire to even contemplate. Jack Kemp, the pro-immigration former congressman, was Dole's running mate. After the 1996 election, O'Sullivan was ousted as *NR* editor.

The right's pundit wars raged on. Sam Francis-style activism was practiced by such organizations as Federation for American Immigration Reform (FAIR), the Carrying Capacity Network (CCN), Numbers USA, and the more scholarly Center for Immigration Studies (CIS). FAIR's Dan Stern made numerous television appearances before hostile hosts. The CCN addressed overpopulation and environmental concerns. These organizations all had grassroots support, with membership in the hundreds of thousands. Francis's work, however, was too controversial for any of them. Publishers, in time, took notice. In 1996, Roy Beck, president of Numbers USA, published *The Case Against Immigration*, devoting two chapters to how mass immigration harms black Americans.

That same year, Williamson brought out *The Immigration Mystique*, boldly claiming that the United States was never intended to become a nation of immigrants. The year before came the blockbuster: Peter Brimelow's *Alien Nation*. Brimelow's argument preceded Williamson's. The Founders, including George Washington, Thomas Jefferson, Alexander Hamilton, and Benjamin Franklin, all held a dim view of immigration. Brimelow also made a moral argument against mass immigration. The American people were told in 1965 that demographic upheaval would never take place. The public never voted for such astronomical numbers.

The surprise was that all three books were published by major New York houses. W.W. Norton for Beck, Basic Books for Williamson, and Random House, the nation's most prestigious firm, for *Alien Nation*. In contrast, Buchanan's 2002 runaway best-seller, *The Death of the West*, was reportedly rejected by five publishing houses before finding a home at Thomas Dunne's imprint at St. Martin's Press.

Sam Francis had no chance for a New York publisher. Or even a university press. *Revolution From The Middle* was published by Middle American Press, an outlet of the Raleigh, N.C.—based monthly. *American Extinguished* was brought out by Center for Immigration Control (CIC). Who would review them? Read them? What bookstore would stock them? What public or university library would pick them up? On immigration, no columnist was more prolific. No columnist, also, was more ostracized.

Does culture precede politics? Would the outburst of intelligent anti-immigration scholarship result in congressional action? More frustration. Senators Gaylord Nelson (D—WI) and Eugene McCarthy (D—MN), both "yes" votes on the 1965 bill, now held regrets. In 1992, McCarthy penned *A Colony of the World*, a modest brief against mass immigration, implying by the title that the United States was now a dumping ground for the Third World.

Nelson tried an environmental argument, lecturing on college campuses. Few takers for this duo. The liberal media would *not* be there for them.

By the early 1980s America had lost its southern border. Republican Senator Alan Simpson (R—WY) and Democratic Congressman Roman Mazzoli (D—KY) crafted a bill to secure the border. The proposed legislation did not address legal immigration nor did it seek to construct a wall or a fence. It only sought to levy fines on employers hiring illegals. During the 1984 presidential debates, Ronald Reagan floated a compromise: border security combined with amnesty for illegal aliens. In 1986, the Simpson-Mazzoli bill passed with bipartisan support. The illegals received amnesty, but the border remained unprotected.

The issue festered. Sam Francis-style politics manifested itself with California's Proposition 187. After 187's overwhelmingly approval, an activist Liberal judge promptly overturned the law. Proposition 187 did get the attention of the Clinton White House. The president appointed former Rep. Barbara Jordan (D—TX) to chair a commission that recommended modest cuts in legal immigration. Any momentum was blunted by Jordan's untimely death in 1996, plus opposition to any restrictionist bill from House Majority Leader Dick Armey (R—TX). In a speech before the libertarian CATO Institute, Armey maintained that not one major economic or social problem had ever occurred from mass immigration.

Most Republican House members voted for immigration restrictions in a bill sponsored by Rep. Lamar Smith (R—TX). Up to 77 members did not. That number, combined with Democratic Party opposition, sank the bill. Those Republican renegades were booed as they left the House floor.

After the 1996 election, Francis declared that paleoconservative-style conservatism was finished. Time to become explicit. He associated with the C of CC and American Renaissance and worked as book page editor for *Occidental Quarterly*, all far right elements that establishment conservatives ignored. Sam also maintained both his syndicated column and his popular monthly *Chronicles* column. Buchanan's political career was over. John O'Sullivan had been fired as editor of *National Review*. Scott McConnell would lose his job as editorial page editor at the *New York Post*. *Wall Street Journal*-style mass immigration policies prevailed.

In 2000, Texas Governor George W. Bush easily won the GOP presidential nomination. As with Bush Senior, "Dubya" was pro-immigration, indeed, militantly so. He scolded Republicans on their opposition to illegal immigration, claiming that "family values" did not stop at the U.S.—Mexico border. Hispanics, GOP operatives claimed, possessed strong family values, making them natural Republicans. Bush spoke Spanish on the stump and even gave a national radio address in that tongue. Bush gloated that America is "now one of the largest Spanish-speaking nations in the world. Just go to Miami or San Antonio, Los Angeles, Chicago or West New York, New Jersey, and close your eyes and listen. You could just as easily be in Santo Domingo or Santiago, or San Miguel de Allende."

Bush was elected president and re-elected. History, however, never stands still. Conservatives were still upset with Bush's pro-immigrant militancy. In 2004, fed-up Arizonians initiated their own version of California's Proposition 187. Arizona's Proposition 204 would require proof of citizenship before registering to vote, photo ID for receiving a ballot, and verification of immigration status before applying for certain public benefits. The proposition was opposed by Arizona's leading newspapers and the state's most popular politician. Senator John McCain, a vocal supporter of illegal alien amnesty, claimed the initiative would do nothing to alleviate the problem. Still, the proposition passed easily.

Sam Francis-style politics was also alive in the nation's capital. The rise of the Immigration Reform Caucus (IRC) was the achievement of Rep. Tancredo, the intrepid congressman who once served in President Reagan's Department of Education in Colorado, where he helped to reduce that state's federal share by 75 percent. In time, the IRC had over 100 GOP House members. By 2005, Tancredo had full reign over the issue. George W. Bush wanted amnesty. The IRC—and the House Republican leadership—balked. A bill cracking down on illegal immigration was passed and signed into law. Tancredo, for reasons unknown, did not seek legal immigration reductions.

And so, the issue remained dormant until being revived by Donald Trump's 2016 campaign.

Democrats were united in support of mass immigration, open borders, and amnesty. Republicans were divided. McCain, Lindsay Graham (R—SC), Jeff Flake (R—AZ), Lisa Murkowski (R—AK), Susan Collins (R—ME) and Rob Portman (R—OH) all took Bush-like positions. In the House, up to 200 Republicans voted for a bill by Judiciary Chairman Robert Goodlatte (R—VA) that would have achieved immigration reductions. It wasn't enough for passage.

Favoring immigration, to Sam Francis, was a prime example of the elites in action. The cheap vote (Democrat), cheap labor (Republican) coalition has held for the past 60 years. Nothing would deter them—not even the worst terrorist attack in American history.

On September 11, 2001, two airliners commandeered by Islamic terrorists crashed into the World Trade Center in New York City and the Pentagon in northern Virginia. A third, on its way to Washington, was thwarted by patriots, led by Todd Beamer, who disarmed the hijackers but could not save United Airlines Flight #93 from crashing into a Pennsylvania cornfield.

In Washington, the Bush Administration was starting to find its legs. The president that day was in Sarasota, Florida, reading to second graders. On September 13, newspapers across America flashed a page one photo of one Mohammad Atta, a native of Egypt, the leader of the terrorist squad. On May 17, Atta, who had been living in Germany on a student visa, applied for—and received—a five-year B-1/B-2 tourist student visa at the United States embassy in Berlin. The hijacker/suicide bombers entered the U.S. legally. On September 11, only two of the 19 terrorists had overstayed their visas. The other 17 were legal residents of the United States.

For Sam Francis the response of the power elites to 9/11 was not surprising. The United States before and after remained "a nation of immigrants." Congress did pass legislation limiting student visas, proposed in 1996 by Rep. Lamar Smith (R—TX). The Smith bill became law—too late to save 3,000 innocent lives. After the attack, President Bush instructed Secretary of State Colin Powell to tell pro-immigration lobbies that nothing would change. The United States would remain a welcoming nation.

On the morning of the attack, Sam was having breakfast at a northern Virginia diner. "It's war," a waitress informed the columnist. The mantra, as Sam related, was the same all over town. Sam's first post 9/11 column was ill-tempered. Joe Sobran's was more mournful. Both men had opposed all of America's post-Cold War conflicts. "I've been warning people for years that our enemies would have some nasty tricks up their sleeves," Sobran lamented. Sam was more defiant. He was as blunt as a steel toe. In the oceans of ink of print and digital words spilled on 9/11 commentary, no column was more devastating. Or angrier. It began with the roots of the current troubles, the 1991 Persian Gulf War, which Sam had opposed:

> The blunt truth is that the United States has been at war for at least a decade, since we launched a war against Iraq in 1991, even though Iraq had done nothing to harm the United States. Our bombing attacks on Iraq certainly caused civilian casualties, and if they were not deliberate, nobody beating the war drums at the time felt much regret for them. For ten years, we have maintained economic sanctions on Iraq that have led to the deaths of hundreds of thousands of civilians, and we have repeatedly bombed it whenever it failed to abide by the standards we imposed on it.

That was just the warmup. Next, a declaration. Here, Francis endorsed the "blowback" theory.

> Someday it might actually dawn on someone in this country that the grown-up, but unwelcome answer is that the terrorists attacked us because they were paying us back for what we started.
>
> Let us hear no more about how the "terrorists" have "declared war on America." Any nation that allows a criminal chief executive [President Clinton] to use its military power to slaughter civilians in unprovoked and legally unauthorized attacks for his own personal political purposes can expect whatever the "terrorists" dish out to it. If we should make no distinction between those who harbor terrorists and those who commit terrorist acts, neither can any distinction be made between those who tolerate the murderous policies of a criminal in power and the criminal itself.
>
> The blunt and ugly truth is that the United States has been at war for years—that it started the war in the name of "spreading democracy," "building nations," "waging peace," "stopping aggression," "enforcing human rights," and all the other pious lies that warmongers always invoke to mask the truth, and that it continued the war simply to save a crook from political ruin. What is new is merely that this week, for the first time, the war we started came home—and all of a sudden, Americans don't seem to care for it much.

The 9/11 attacks represented a defining moment. Sam's eloquence was up to the task of explaining the real meaning:

> September 11 changed absolutely nothing, and the reason it did not is precisely because of what I have repeatedly argued in columns—the lack of

immigration control is not simply a passing whim or a romantic delusion that can be dispelled by a dose of cold reality.

Mass immigration is a deliberate, politically created policy, deeply rooted in the material interests of the ruling elites of the United States. It serves to depress wages and lower labor costs for large corporations; it serves to replenish a dwindling number of members in labor unions, it offers entire new constituencies and voting blocs to the two established political parties; it provides a new underclass for which an immense welfare bureaucracy can deliver services and social therapy; and it promises a new "multicultural" and "multiracial" society in which cultural elites, already deeply alienated from traditional American and Western institutions, and vast new ethnic lobbies can gain power.

When a policy is as closely entwined with material interests—money and power—as immigration is now, it tends to become impervious to ideas and arguments, and it will take more than the terrorism of September 11—let alone newspaper columns, books, and speeches—to change it.

On immigration, Sam Francis was at his freewheeling best. There were political and economic consequences—the obliteration of the Nixon-Reagan coalition—and ever-sinking wages. Sam's view was apocalyptic. Who cares about the Republican Party when the historic America was disappearing right in front of the eyes? Sam hit the immigration issue on all fronts: American and Western history, the peoples' sovereignty, free speech, poverty, crime, disease. Several columns in *America Extinguished* are devoted to the Columbus Day controversy. Why attack Christopher Columbus? He brought European civilization to the New World. That's reason enough. Crime? Francis didn't hesitate to tackle the issue of immigrant crime, notably an incident in Minnesota where a Hmong immigrant killed a slew of white hunters. The story was not just the crime, but the negligent media reaction. The situation became worse after Sam penned these columns.

Francis's arguments can be described under several headings:

National unity. The American motto is *E Pluribus Unum* (from many, one). Politicians from across the spectrum have wrongly interpreted that motto as meaning of many people, one nation, making it an excuse for more immigration. What it *does* means, Francis reminded readers, is that out of 13 colonies, there is one nation. The United States was never intended to become the thing causing so much anxiety, a multicultural nation.

Democracy. During the 1990s, such Midwestern Republicans as Spencer Abraham of Michigan and Mike DeWine of Ohio prevented the Republican senate from approving immigration reductions. Every ten years, however, Michigan and Ohio lose congressional seats and Electoral College votes to such high immigrant states as Texas and Florida. The results? Congressional districts populated by American citizens are lost to newly created ones where many, if not most, residents are illegals or immigrants who never bother earning citizenship. "High immigration," Francis reported, quoting from the Center of Immigration Studies (CIS), "produces a situation in which American citizens lose representation in Congress so that non-citizen immigrants, none of whom can vote and many of whom are illegal, can be 'represented' in the House."

Language. By 1990, there were up to 32 million people in the United States speaking in foreign tongues. As Sam reported from a story in his old employer the *Washington Times*: "There has been a widely reported surge in the growth of special ethnic language schools teaching Persian, Hindi, Mandarin, Korean, Farsi, Czech and other languages to immigrant youth. They offer a way for immigrant parents to instill in their youngsters the parents' native culture and tradition while keeping their offspring from total assimilation into U.S. citizens." Again, the year. 1990.

Free speech. In 1999, Craig Nelson paid for a billboard in Queens County, New York asking: "Tired of being stuck in traffic? Every day the U.S. Congress lets in 6,000 immigrants. Every day." Free speech in action? Local politicians immediately denounced the billboard. They declared their support for free speech, just not *this* free speech. City Council President Peter Vallone announced that there was "no room for messages of hatred on billboards." The message was removed and as Francis contended, so too were Mr. Nelson's rights.

Ethnic separatism. A "Chicano separatists" movement evolved in the Southwest. By 2000, one Charles Truxillo, professor of Chicano Studies at the University of New Mexico, maintained that decades hence, when Latinos are the clear majority in that region, they should "reclaim [their] birthright by any means necessary— and not shy away." Earlier in Sam's column, "Ethnic Separatism Threatens America," he quoted the professor: Mexicans "are a people with a country that has been taken from them by war, a land that was ours by our own treaty." Hence, the *reconquista*.

Poverty. By 2000, of the 35 million Americans living in poverty, 26 percent were immigrants. "There would be more than nine million fewer poor people in this country if immigration had been halted," Francis declared.

Disease. During the immigrant-heavy 1990s, tuberculous in the United States declined. According to the Center for Disease Control, it increased among the immigrant population. In California, 70 percent of TB cases were from immigrants. In New York, 53 percent of such cases were from the same demographic. TB is a death-causing disease.

Why did America surrender? Was there an historical factor? Did the great conflicts of 1914 to 1919 and 1939 to 1945 zap the fight out of Western man? Had the West fought itself into exhaustion? Had Americans succumbed to the politics of intimidation? Had they surrendered to the smears of "racism"? Had they become spoiled by the welfare state? The television set? Can the West survive Adolf Hitler? Sam believed in a republic. That comes with responsibilities.

Americans lacked the will to fight back. From a landmark essay, "Nationalism Old and New," Sam laid out a seemingly contradictory position:

> Men who become dependent on others cannot govern themselves, and if they cannot govern themselves, they cannot keep a republic. Today, virtually everyone in the United States is habituated to a style of living that is wrapped up in dependency on mass organizations—supermarkets, hospitals, insurance companies, the bureaucratized police, local government, the mass media, the factories and office buildings where we work, the apartment complexes and suburban communities where we live, and the massive, remote, and mysterious national state that supervises almost every detail of our lives.
>
> Most Americans cannot even imagine life without such dependencies and would not want to live without them. The classical republicans were right. Having become dependent on others for our livelihoods, our protection, our entertainment, and even our thoughts and tastes, we are corrupted. We neither want a republic nor could we keep it if we had one. We do not deserve to have one, and like the barbarians conquered and enslaved by the Greeks and Romans, we are suited only for servitude.

Yet such people, under siege from the managerial revolution, could form the backbone of the opposition. Why?

> Even though no one today subscribes to the classical republican ideal of virtue and independence, there remain a large number of Americans whose material

interests and most deeply held cultural codes are endangered by the national managerial regime.

These "Middle Americans" largely white and middle class, derive their income from their dependence on the mass structures of the managerial economy, and because many of them have long since lost their habits of self-reliance, they also are dependent on the services of the government and the dominant culture.

Yet despite their dependency, the regime does little for them and much to them. They find that their jobs are insecure, their savings stripped of value, their neighborhoods and schools unsafe, their elected leaders indifferent and often crooked, their moral beliefs and religious professions and social codes under perpetual attack even from their own government, their children taught to despise what they believe, their very identity and heritage as a people threatened, and their future—political, economic, cultural, racial, national, and personal—uncertain.

They find that no matter what party or candidate they support, no matter what the candidates and parties promise, nothing substantially changes, except for the worse. Although they do the labor that sustains the managerial system, pay the taxes that support it, fight the wars its leaders devise, raise the families and try to pass on the beliefs and habits that enable the regime and the country to survive and exist, what they receive from the regime is never commensurate with what they give it.

A tall order. A people "only fit for servitude" must now rebel to the point that even the Republican Party would pay attention. In some cases the people did respond, i.e., propositions in both California and Arizona. So, too, did politicians in such state legislatures as Georgia, Oklahoma, and Arizona with crackdowns on the illegal population. The Republican Party, meanwhile, had its priorities all wrong. Instead of "Economic Man" policies like tax and spending reductions, the party needed to satisfy its working-class base: no to free trade; yes to the immigration moratorium, sealed borders, and legislation that would have illegals self-deport.

In response to nearly unlimited immigration, Sam Francis spoke. As did Sam Francis-style grassroots politics: CCN, FAIR, Numbers USA, Americans for Immigration Control, California's Proposition 187, Arizona's Proposition 204. Francis, virtually alone, wanted to create a white racial unity. For post-civil rights America, an impossibility. The economic argument is the only viable option. Mass immigration sinks real wages for the workingman. Undeterred, Sam Francis plowed forward. He had allies. Still, immigration became another lonely struggle. With open borders, family reunification, birthright citizenship, demographic upheaval, and the assaults on American history, the United States, that pre-1965 happy, content, ever-confident nation had disappeared from the face of the earth.

13.

A Prophet Is Proved Right

THE CAMPAIGNS OF DONALD TRUMP, beginning in 2016, were a resurgence of Sam Francis politics. A decade after his death, there was a revival of Sam's worldview.

During Trump's rise, Buchanan's career was resurrected. A week after Trump was elected, Michael Brendan Dougherty, who had earlier penned a negative essay on Sam's career, revisited his old subject. Writing for *The Week*, Dougherty recalled Francis's advice to Buchanan when the latter was set to run for the 1992 GOP presidential nomination: Go to New Hampshire and call yourself a patriot, a nationalist, an America Firster, never a conservative. Trumpism was a variation of Buchananism with exceptions: no to free trade and "nation of immigrants" ideology but without emphasizing social issues like abortion and gay marriage. Instead, protect jobs and the border and stay out of foreign wars. Dougherty wrote that Francis was an "obscure adviser to Pat Buchanan."

There was more. In January 2016, Rush Limbaugh excitedly read an excerpt from a Francis essay articulating a right-wing populist platform. Podcaster Tucker Carlson used "anarcho-tyranny" on air, although without attribution. A recent book (*When the Clock Broke* by John Ganz) presents a very negative view of the populist uprisings of the 1990s but treats Sam Francis as a major figure.

David Brooks also acknowledged Francis's enduring appeal. In a September 22, 2017 column, Brooks, who once worked with Sam at the *Washington Times*, explained Francis's worldview to his liberal readers. Brooks admitted that when he worked for the *Times* in the late 1980s, he thought Sam "was a crank." But he was wrong. ["It's] clear now that he was becoming one of the most prescient writers for the past 50 years." Brooks complemented Dougherty's analysis:

> In a series of essays for *Chronicles*, Francis hammered home three key insights. The first was that globalization was screwing Middle America. The Cold War had just ended, capitalism seemed triumphant and the Clinton years seemed to be an era of broad prosperity. But Francis stressed that a service economy was ruining small farms and taking jobs from the working class. His second insight was that the Republican and conservative establishment did not understand what was happening. He railed against the pro-business "Economic Men" who thought G.D.P. growth could solve the nation's problems, and the Washington Republicans, who he thought were infected with the values of the educated elites. His third insight was that politics was no longer about left versus right. Instead, a series of smaller conflicts — religious versus secular, nationalist versus globalist, white versus nonwhite — were all merging into a larger polarity, ruling class versus Middle America.

The kicker? A Republican Party that, shockingly enough, would become even more nationalist:

> Trump is nominally pro-business. The next populism will probably take his ethnic nationalism and add an anti-corporate, anti-tech layer. Google, Facebook, Amazon, and Apple stand for everything Francis hated—economically, culturally, demographically, and nationalistically. As the tech behemoths intrude more deeply into daily life and our very minds, they

will become a defining issue in American politics. It wouldn't surprise me if a new demagogue emerged, one that is even more pure Francis.

Demagogue? Francis's immense scholarship snuffs out that claim. On immigration, the GOP was not yet a Trump-Buchanan-Francis party. During Trump's first term, immigration, legal and illegal plummeted. Following the COVID-19 virus outbreak, Trump, through executive order, even slapped a moratorium on legal immigration.

The Republican congress did nothing to assist Trump's uphill battle. House Speaker Paul Ryan (R—WI) was a former aide to Jack Kemp and a militant supporter of legal immigration. He opposed any reductions. Mitch McConnell, now Senate Majority Leader, didn't care. He made tepid positive comments towards restrictionist legislation introduced by Senators Tom Cotton (R—ARK) and David Perdue (R—GA). That was it.

Democrats were united in support of mass immigration, open borders, and amnesty. Republicans were divided. McCain, Lindsay Graham (R—SC), Jeff Flake (R—AZ), Lisa Murkowski (R—AK), Susan Collins (R—ME), and Rob Portman (R—OH) all took Bush-like positions. In the House, up to 200 Republicans voted for a bill by Judiciary Chairman Robert Goodlatte (R—VA) that would have achieved Sam Francis-style reductions. After the bill failed, Goodlatte bitterly criticized Ryan for the latter's lack of support.

In 2020, Trump lost a disputed re-election bid to Joseph R. Biden. Despite trailing heavily in the polls, Trump made the race close. The latter lost the Electoral College vote in Georgia, Arizona, and Wisconsin by a combined 43,000-vote margin. Victory in all three states would have given Trump a stunning re-election win.

Claiming voter fraud, the Trump team filed numerous lawsuits. On Jan. 6, 2021, Trump hoped that Vice President Mike Pence would not certify the presidential vote so that certain legal actions may proceed. Pence did certify and a riotous day on Capitol Hill began. Trump's January 6 speech called for peaceful protests. An army of his supporters stormed the Capitol, even occupying the House Speaker's chair. Trump was promptly impeached for a second time. The Senate acquitted. Trump's political career was declared over. Except it wasn't. The GOP rank and file remained faithful. In 2024, Trump vanquished his rivals, including popular Florida Governor Ron DeSantis, to claim a third consecutive presidential nomination.

The 2024 election year was like no other. It mirrored the tumult that had overtaken a once-tranquil nation. In late 2023 Trump pulled ahead of Biden in public opinion polling. The Biden Administration, wracked by open borders, inflation, and wars in Eastern Europe and the Middle East, was failing badly. At an August rally in Butler, Pennsylvania, Trump survived an assassination attempt. Two more plots were uncovered. After a successful GOP convention in Milwaukee, Biden dropped out of the race while endorsing Vice President Kamala Harris. The latter enjoyed a Barack Obama-like boost from a relieved media.

Trump's 2024 campaign was pure Sam Francis. It was as if Francis had been reincarnated as a Donald Trump speechwriter. On foreign policy, Trump remained unabashedly America First, promising to end conflicts in Eastern Europe and the Middle East, while swearing that NATO countries would begin paying their fair share of that organization's defense burden. On trade, Trump maintained that "tariff" was now the most beautiful word in the English language.

The GOP convention floor was swamped with "Mass Deportation Now" placards. At a raucous sold-out rally at New York's Madison Square Garden, Trump declared that the United States was now an "occupied country." On the culture front, Trump mounted his own Southern strategy, promising to restore the original names of military bases in the region—Fort Lee, Fort A.P. Hill, Fort Bragg, Fort Hood, among others—that were renamed during the Biden years. Also striking were omissions on certain social issues. Trump's GOP was going all-out on the nationalist agenda.

As in 2016 and 2020, the polls significantly underestimated Trump's final margin. The election ended with Trump winning the popular vote by six million ballots, scoring a 49-47 percent victory.

Times had changed. It wasn't the old Nixon-Reagan coalition. The abortion issue had moved college-educated white women into the Democratic Party camp. "Non-college" whites remained overwhelmingly Republican. Up to 80 percent of non-college white males voted for Trump. Overall, 52 percent of white women voted for Trump, while 59 of all white males did the same. This represented a slight decrease of the entire white vote from previous elections. Trump's free-wheeling style proved popular with male Latinos (54 percent Republican) and male blacks, who checked in with a more modest 21 percent. The revolution of the beefy worker guys remained in full force. In addition, 81 percent of white evangelicals voted for Trump. Once at the center of American politics, this demographic, along with white non-college voters, had disappeared from extensive media scrutiny.

Sam Francis's Middle American Radicals came through again. Trump flipped six states from 2020: Georgia, Arizona, Nevada, Wisconsin, Michigan, and Pennsylvania. In the 37 states of the Pennsylvania to Nevada fly-over country, Trump carried 31 of them, giving him his 312 electoral college victory.

When Samuel T. Francis passed away in early 2005, there was a nasty commentary by one David Mastio in the *Washington Examiner*. That was all. Even though Sam had been ill for weeks, his family, friends, colleagues and nationwide army of readers were bereaved. Paul Gottfried counseled the conservative media to be respectable. This was no time to denounce the man. Gottfried's wish was honored. Respectable establishment conservatives were silent. No mention of Sam's death appeared in *National Review, Weekly Standard, Wall Street Journal, American Spectator,* or *Commentary*.

There was one conservative publication that had to respond. On February 16, 2005, a day after Francis's passing, the *Washington Times* published an obituary. It listed Sam's accomplishments:

Distinguished Writing Awards for editorial writing from the American Society of Newspaper Editors and his work at the Heritage Foundation and for Senator East. It quoted Mary Lou Forbes, commentary editor of the *Times*:

> I remember Sam as a scholarly, challenging and sometimes pungent writer, who distinguished his craft with a remarkable appreciation of history and literature. In person, his witty and sage observations of the passing scene brightened the atmosphere where he labored.

The *Washington Times* considers itself a major voice of American conservatism. The obituary, likewise, couldn't resist taking a dig at Sam's reactionary views:

> Mr. Francis frequently expressed provocative views on topics of history, race and culture that were often contested by other conservatives. "Mass immigration means revolution, the displacement of one people and its culture by others." On the 40th anniversary of the 1954 *Brown v. Board of Education* ruling which declared mandated segregated public schools unconstitutional, Mr. Francis called it "the most dangerous and destructive Supreme Court decision in American history."

In his last column, published Jan. 27, Mr. Francis criticized President Bush's second inaugural address: "The president confirmed once and for all that the neoconservatism to which he has delivered his administration and the country is fundamentally indistinguishable" from liberalism.

Several days later, the *Washington Post* chipped in. The editors most likely had read the *Times'* obituary and apparently decided to follow suit. The obit was a hastily put-together affair. It wasn't especially original. From the *Post:*

> Over the years, Mr. Francis wrote about terrorism, race, immigration, education, and other issues that, as his Web site proclaimed, "no other nationally syndicated columnist, left or right, would touch." His column on the 40th anniversary of the 1954 school desegregation decision in *Brown v. Board of Education* was an apt example. He described the ruling as "the most dangerous and destructive Supreme Court decision in American history." In his final column, published Jan. 27, Mr. Francis's principled disdain was on vivid display. He took issue with President Bush's second inaugural address. Bush, he wrote, "confirmed once and for all that the neo-conservatism to which he has delivered his administration and the country is fundamentally indistinguishable from the liberalism many conservatives imagine he has renounced and defeated."

The Washington Post was plenty aware of Sam Francis. Did they not publish Dinesh D'Souza's attack? His final column had excoriated Bush's second inaugural address. Imagine, a conservative blasting the right-wing Bush! Even more eye-opening was Sam's column criticizing the *Brown* decision. During the 1950s and '60s, conservative opposition to *Brown* was common. But 50 years after the fact? *The Post* could not believe that such a man still existed. "He wasn't just conservative but proudly 'paleoconservative' — certainly not neoconservative," it stated. That was most true.

Sam Francis was not a pessimist. In a 1995 interview with *Southern Partisan*, he said, "I believe I am an optimist" over the future of right-wing populism. If pessimism prevailed, how could Sam be so prolific? In his 1948 classic, *Ideas Have Consequences*, Richard Weaver wrote: "Individuals die. Cultures die. So do nations and civilizations.... We have to inform the multitude that restoration comes at a price.... Do you see the necessity of accepting duties before you begin to talk of freedom? These things will be very hard."

Sam Francis, I believe, would agree with this. Here are the final lines of his *America Extinguished*: "Americans who read these columns and agree with their drift cannot afford to wait for sitting politicians to stop sitting and take action. If we ourselves are not willing to do what is necessary, we have no right to expect anyone else to do it for us."

At the 2004 JRC conference, Scott P. Richert, *Chronicles* managing editor, was in attendance. He was joined there by his wife. Afterwards, a mutual friend approached the couple. "Does Sam always smile so much?" she asked. "He was the happiest person here!" Richert continued:

> At a previous John Randolph Club in Georgetown, I had the honor of introducing Sam, and, in my remarks, I said that, under this gruff exterior, there was a cuddly teddy bear. I was playing the line for laughs, but, by that time, I'd come to know Sam well enough to realize that there was more truth than not in my joke.

Teddy bear? Sam Francis? The scourge of political correctness? Of liberalism? Conservatism, too? All so true. At San Antonio, Sam was relaxed, even upbeat.

Beyond America, Francis wrote occasionally about right wing populism in Europe. Columns praised Jean-Marie Le Pen, longtime leader of France's *Front National* (now *Rassemblement*

National) as that country's Ronald Reagan. Others cited Italy's Silvio Berlusconi's successful efforts to stem the tide of illegal immigration into that culturally rich nation. Most European countries now are home to right wing parties that embrace Francis-like positions on trade, immigration, and non-interventionism. To the bitter chagrin of Western elites, voters in Italy, Hungary, and Poland have elected right-wing leaders as prime ministers. In others, such parties are kept out of governments by a left-right *cordon sanitarie*.

When Francis died, the populist phenomenon was not a serious force. In recent years, Hungary's Viktor Orban has become a favorite for frustrated American and European populists. Sam would have supported Orban's success, plus those of Marine Le Pen, Giorgina Meloni, and Poland's Law and Justice Party.

Sam Francis never gave into despair. Near the end of his James Burnham biography, Sam quoted his subject, "The past is determined, but for human beings the future is free. It is too early to publish the West's obituary." Thanks to the Sam Francis-style politics practiced in many countries the West does indeed have a fighting chance.

The secret to Sam Francis's ongoing relevance?

He reveled in a right-wing populism pitting the heartland against the political, economic, academic, and media elites. So, too, did Pat Buchanan and Donald Trump. On a higher level, Francis brought into battle a thorough knowledge of American and Western history. Consequently, his opinion had plenty of muscle behind it. Francis understood that it is lust for power that prevails in the hearts of men. Better, as he once wrote, for conservatives to be the hammer than the anvil.

We are not finished with Samuel T. Francis. Not by a long shot. In fairness, his emphasis on race was, at first, a defensive reaction to anti-Western multiculturalism. It also represented old-fashioned tribalism. Try as it might, liberal democracy cannot vanquish tribalism, itself a stubborn fact of history. Sam fought his battles through the prism of Christian morality. Reactionary change was needed. It would come through means peaceful and democratic.

He was utterly fearless in his convictions. Francis didn't enjoy being ostracized. He was willing to pay the price, supported as he was by an army of loyal readers. Thomas Fleming maintains that *pietas* towards the man's old stock American ancestry inspired his often-lonely stand. Sam Francis was a son of the American Revolution and the Confederacy. When that heritage was assaulted: Thomas Jefferson here, Robert E. Lee there, Sam sprang into action.

In doing so, he inspired others to walk towards that same fire. His legacy of courage shines with increasing brilliance. His unmistakable voice will resonate in the decades and centuries ahead.

14.

Francis At Rest

IN HIS FINAL COLUMNS in both *Chronicles* and in his syndicated dispatches, Sam remained steadfast: Blunt, eloquent, far-reaching. He defended Harvard University President Lawrence Summers from charges of sexism when the latter acknowledged that male students scored better in mathematics than their female counterparts. He wondered if Russell Kirk's "politics of prudence" was the right formula for taking on a militant leftism. As noted, he roundly criticized President Bush's second inaugural address for supporting democratic movements worldwide with the pie-in-the-sky notion of "ending tyranny in our world."

Sam's final *Chronicles* column covered a familiar theme. The managerial state told their subjects how to think, act, and feel. Likewise, "anarcho-tyranny" allowed the government to pursue a policy of endless wars and open borders while harassing and demonizing anyone who dared object to the regime. Sam's examples included an unprovoked war in Iraq by a government that refuses to defend its borders and uses hidden cameras to catch and fine speeding motorists in the Washington, D.C. area, while a Somali immigrant working in a nearby retirement home slashes away at both hapless patients and a fellow worker:

> What we have in this country is both anarchy (the failure of the state to enforce the laws) and, at the same time, tyranny—the enforcement of laws by the state for oppressive purposes; the criminalization

of the law-abiding and innocent through exorbitant taxation, bureaucratic regulation, the invasion of privacy, and the engineering of social institutions, such as the family and local schools; the imposition of thought control through "sensitivity training" and multiculturalist curricula, "hate crime" laws, gun-control laws that punish or disarm otherwise law-abiding citizens but have no impact on violent criminals, who get guns illegally, and a vast labyrinth of other measures. In a word, *anarcho-tyranny*.

In December 2004, Sam made his final public appearance, giving an address at the annual John Randolph Club conference. That winter it was held in San Antonio. Some humour was involved. Local leftists got wind of the event. They traveled to the lodgings where the conference was being held and picketed, all with the usual chants and noise. Why? Well, the malcontents claimed that the JRC members "had ties" to the Bush Administration. That got a good chuckle from Tom Fleming and other attendees.

Sam was in a good mood. By now he had learned to lecture without a prepared text. He saw some hope from the 2004 results. Bush, incompetence aside, won all but five states (Illinois, Minnesota, Michigan, Wisconsin, and Pennsylvania) in Willmoore Kendall fly over country. The MARS coalition had legs to it. Moreover, Sam felt that the patriotic support of the Iraq War was a good sign. That might be transferred to other issues, such as immigration and trade. Immigration hawk Tom Tancredo was easily re-elected to Congress and Arizona's Proposition 204, despite opposition from Senator McCain, was overwhelmingly approved. At the Christmas season, Sam was at ease, among readers and fans.

Sam was a man, unknowingly, at the end of a long journey. For over 30 years, he had fought the good fight in the outer jungles of modernism. On a daily basis, he battled a world both alien and hostile. He would leave behind a body of work to be read, analyzed, and enjoyed by generations yet born. A teddy bear? You bet! For one weekend, Sam was at home, among people who loved him, who would stand with him forever, who would be grateful to have known such a man during this brief existence. Sam Francis was happy, among friends.

In late January, Sam suffered his first heart seizure. He called for an ambulance. None arrived. He got into his car and drove to a Seabrook hospital. Sam immediately went through seven hours of emergency surgery for an aortic aneurysm. Doctors feared it was life-threatening. Sam stayed on sedation for days, where he received friends. Physicians were afraid that Francis would not survive any movement. They were correct. A team of doctors did try to pick him up from his bed-ridden position. Sam was too weak. That simple movement caused his death. Sam Francis was 57.

Upon Sam's passing, word spread quickly. A beloved colleague had died before his time. Even if Sam Francis had lived and never published another word, comrades and friends would cherish him.

Some tributes were brief, others were longer. All were heartfelt. Fittingly, it was Tom Fleming, Sam's greatest champion, who delivered the news:

> It is with unspeakable regret that I have to report the death of my friend and colleague Sam Francis. In any age, he would have been a remarkable man for the penetration of his mind, his unflinching pursuit of truth—regardless of current cant or personal consequences—and the gravity of his style. In our age, he is peerless, and his death represents an irreplaceable loss.
>
> Sam and I were friends and allies for over 25 years. A gentleman of a school so old we can no longer recognize its existence, Sam never talked of his "feelings" and if one spoke of loyalty or friendship, he was sure to make an ironic quip. Nonetheless, I learned early on that he was loyal to his friends

even (especially) when it entailed a threat to his own interest. In so many ways, he was the opposite of most conservatives. He rarely talked a good game, but he always played one.

Clyde Wilson, Southern historian, conjured up a Tennessee connection:

> Like his fellow Tennessean General Nathan Bedford Forrest, 'He bought a one-way ticket to the war.' That means that Forrest, once committed to a good cause—the defense of his people—devoted his all to the cause and never looked back. Such a man was Sam Francis.

And Chilton Williamson, Jr. Sam and Chilton spent many hours on the phone, conversing from their respective homes in Kemmerer, Wyoming, and Seabrook, Maryland. Chilton would pour a glass of wine and the two would happily ruminate on a world gone mad. Chilton wrote, "It is strange to look at that telephone and realize that I will never again hear Sam's voice on the line."

Other tributes only needed one sentence:

"We shall not see his like again." Roger McGrath.

"The enemies of our civilization can breathe a sigh of relief." Srdja Trifkovic.

Others came from official headquarters. From Vladimir Palko, Minister of the Interior, Slovak Republic:

> I was deeply saddened to learn of Samuel Francis's sudden death. His brilliant essays were well known to me. His views and comments on conservatism, religion, and current culture-war issues were both valuable and impressive, and one could get to know

his character through them. Mr. Francis' death is a great loss, and he will be missed by his colleagues and friends, as well as his readers.

Closer to home, were Joe Sobran and Jared Taylor. First, Sobran, comparing Sam to James Burnham:

> Samuel Francis, whose column has appeared in *The Wanderer* for years, has died at 57. One of the most trenchant conservative pens in America will write no more.
>
> Along the way Sam wrote a few books, including a study of James Burnham. I worked with Jim at *National Review* during his last years there and shared Sam's admiration for him.
>
> The key to Sam's thinking was Burnham's book *The Machiavellians,* a study of power I also regard as seminal. Long before it became fashionable to mock the "politically correct," Sam was attracted by Burnham's pessimistic logic and total scorn for liberal optimism. Like Burnham, he had no desire to be accepted by liberals and stoically endured their ostracism. He was devoid of self-pity. It never crossed his mind to complain about the neglect he received, though it was a sort of organized neglect; his enemies were well aware of him, and they feared his pen.
>
> Willmoore Kendall used to say that American conservatives carried their political tradition implicitly, "in their hips." He might have had Sam in mind when he said that. Given his pessimistic temperament, Sam wasn't given to inspiring affirmation. His outlook was bleak. The news was always bad, and I sometimes wondered what, if anything, he would regard as good news. His disdain for Republicans — "the stupid

party," he always called them — was fathomless. He seemed neither surprised nor disappointed when so-called conservatives rallied behind George W. Bush and the Iraq war; Burnham had taught him how deluding political labels and professed principles can be in the realm of power.

As his readers know, Sam Francis rejected false optimism in any form. If there is one Christian doctrine he would have believed without much argument, it is the doctrine of original sin.

Taylor's tribute was especially moving. Where would *American Renaissance* be without Sam's energy?

> Of Sam's brilliance and boldness as a thinker and writer there can be no doubt. He was undoubtedly the premier thinker and philosopher of white racial consciousness of our time. He was a man who could have built an impressive career as a public intellectual if he had been willing to trim his sails and steer between the buoys. This was not Sam's way, and by writing forcefully about what he knew to be true, he sacrificed prominence and acclaim for the greater reward of doing what he saw to be his duty.
>
> And so it is for both professional and personal reasons that I mourn the passing of a great mind and a good friend. It has not yet entirely sunken in to me that this brilliant man is no longer with us. Those of us who shared his vision will carry on, as best we can, without him.

In the days following Sam's death, friends debated on how the man met his end. In his moving eulogy, Tom Fleming was convinced that Sam died as a Christian. Paul Gottfried, whose farewell was just as heartfelt, had his doubts. Was Sam Francis received into the Roman Catholic Church? Upon learning of Sam's life-threatening illness, Christopher Check, president of the Rockford Institute, called his younger brother, a Catholic priest, to see if he could attend to Sam. Check's brother was busy, but he did contact the Rev. Paul Scalia, a priest in the Washington, D.C. area. There was powerful symbolism at work. Rev. Scalia, son of Anton Scalia, the most articulate conservative on the Supreme Court, administering to the most uncompromising conservative columnist in the land.

Sam was born into the Presbyterian Church. In his capacity as an intellectual founder of modern right-wing populism in the United States, Sam traveled in an eclectic circle. The Rockford contingent admired the courage of the old Christendom: Charles Martel, Jan Sobieski, the victors in the Battle of Lepanto. Others embraced paganism, convinced that Christians had turned Western man into a bag of mush, guilt-ridden weaklings who surrendered their nations to the Global South multi-millions.

Sam Francis believed that there was more to Christianity than national suicide. He admired M. Stanton Evans's *The Theme Is Freedom*, a polemic arguing that Christianity with its emphasis on self-denial and full adulthood served as the keystone to true liberty. In his columns, Sam defended the Crusades of long ago.

Sam Francis will be forever linked to Pat Buchanan. Surely, Buchanan and Francis are the two shining greats the postwar conservative movement has ever produced. Their careers, from the 1990's onward, are parallel: With his opposition to the Persian Gulf War, Buchanan was read out of a conservative movement he had sustained for years. In terms of fame, Buchanan was second only to William F. Buckley, Jr. Buchanan's career was laser-like focused on one main objective: the survival and triumph of a Western, Christian civilization. The younger Francis was part of American conservatism only briefly. As with Buchanan, his prolific output kept him a force to be reckoned with. As important, Sam was the ally Buchanan needed at a crucial point in the latter's career. Buchanan's tribute must be published in full:

At the foot of Lookout Mountain, we buried Sam Francis today. A shy, private man, Sam would have been embarrassed by how many would travel here to pay final respects. His Tennessee family told friends who came from all over the country that they had not really known how admired and beloved Sam was.

When God created him, He endowed Sam with a great gift—one of the finest minds of his generation. Sam did not waste it. As a student, he was a prodigy. By high school, he was winning citywide competitions in poetry and essay-writing. From Chattanooga, Sam went on to Johns Hopkins and, from there, to earn a Ph.D. in English history at the University of North Carolina.

Sam then came north to work for the Heritage Foundation, where he became an expert on international terror. He left to join Sen. John East, whose election had folks chortling that Jesse Helms was now "the liberal senator from North Carolina."

Then, Sam took up his real vocation, journalism, joining the *Washington Times*, where he was soon winning national prizes for the quality of his editorials. Sam became a rising star in the conservative firmament and began to write a national column. And that's when Sam got into trouble.

For the founding fathers of the conservative movement had passed on, their estate had gone to probate, and squatters and hustlers had swindled the Old Right out of its inheritance. Soon, others began to redefine conservatism, to impose limits on debate, to censor as heretics those who would not mouth the new party line.

In 1995, Sam merrily ridiculed Baptist churchmen who had issued an apology for slavery. As the preachers had never owned slaves and there was no Bible command against slavery, Sam asked, what exactly were the preachers apologizing for?

Cautioned to watch his step, he did not. For Sam cared about his convictions more than his popularity. As Minister Michael Milton of First Presbyterian eulogized at his gravesite, Sam was one with Flannery O'Connor in believing that "truth does not change according to our ability to stomach it."

Among the events that altered Sam's life was the savaging of his friend and mentor, Mel Bradford, whom Ronald Reagan had chosen to chair the National Endowment for the Humanities. Neoconservatives had coveted the post and the honors a chairman could bestow. So a small cabal painted Bradford, a well-known scholar-critic of Lincoln, as a racist.

"If they want it that bad," Mel told a friend, "let them have it."

Seeing how wounded Bradford had been, Sam was always there when one of his own was caught out in the open. Like his forebears in the Army of the Confederacy, Sam rode to the sound of the guns.

A proud "paleo," he mocked the neo-orthodoxy that the South was always wrong, Wilson and FDR had been right, and Dr. King was a paragon of virtue and patriotism. He delighted in mocking the tin gods of the New and Revised Conservative Bible.

What he cherished was the civilization and culture that had nurtured him. He loved Southern and American literature, history and heroes, and few men of his time were so widely read. Sam was convinced Western culture and civilization could not survive the dispossession or death of the European peoples who gave them birth. He opposed the mass immigration of non-Western peoples, cultures and creeds, and regarded as the "Stupid Party" a GOP that truckled to corporate contributors and refused to defend our borders.

A decade ago, Sam said as much at a conference and was gone from the paper.

He never fully understood what he had done wrong. Said Milton:

"Dr. Francis' defense of the truth led many to admire him, befriend him and, at times, withdraw from him. The work of a prophet is a lonely calling."

With his intelligence, vast knowledge and droll wit, Sam was the most entertaining of dinner companions. His barbs and anecdotes about friends and adversaries had those at his table laughing so loud that other patrons in the restaurant wondered what was going on.

His death was a difficult one. Sam awoke at home on Saturday late in January feeling terrible. No ambulance would come. So, he drove himself to the nearest hospital, where he underwent seven hours of surgery for an aortic aneurysm. Heavily sedated for weeks, as doctors feared he could not survive movement, Sam's heart gave out when they tried to help him sit up in a chair.

I only spoke to Sam for minutes in those final days of his life. And my words here are too long delayed. But Sam's passing has left a hole in our hearts as it will in our lives.

It is difficult to bear the thought I will not again see Sam's big grin, as he sat down to dinner, spread a napkin over his ample lap and proceeded to divest himself of the latest witticisms he had invented.

May the Lord have mercy on my brave and generous friend.

Notes

1. OUR MAN IN SWAMPVILLE. Jared Taylor's tribute in "Sam Francis, R.I.P.," *American Renaissance*, Feb. 16, 2005.

2. ALLIES. John Zmirak's comments in *American Conservatism: An Encyclopedia* (Wilmington: ISI Books. 2006), p. 263. Sam Francis's early poetry in *The Occidental Quarterly*, Summer 2005, p. 20. Information on Sam Francis's participation in conservative organizations supplied in correspondence with Thomas Fleming, Clyde N. Wilson, John Shelton Reed, and Jerry Woodruff. Paul Gottfried's tribute in his *Encounters: My Life with Nixon, Marcuse, and Other Friends and Teachers.* (Wilmington: ISI Books, 2009), p. 157.

3. HIGH HOPES. Louis March's recollections in "Remembering Sam Francis," presented at a memorial program on March 15, 2005, in Arlington, Virginia. Tom Fleming's praise in "Requiescat in Pace, Domini," *Chronicles*, April 2005, p. 25. Sam Francis's Bradford eulogy in "The Legacy of M.E. Bradford," 1993, Tribune Media Services. Samuel T. Francis, "Equality As A Political Weapon," in *Essays in Political Economy, No. 10* (Auburn, Alabama: Ludwig Von Mises Institute), a lecture delivered at Conference on Equality and the Free Society, Princeton, N.J., April 13, 1991.

4. BURNHAMITE. M.E. Bradford's plea is in "Not in Memoriam, But in Affirmation," in *Why the South Will Survive,* pp. 202-210.

5. BEAUTIFUL LOSERS. On McCarthyism: "The Evil That Men Don't Do: Joe McCarthy and the American Right," *Chronicles*, Sept. 1986, pp. 16-21. The appreciation of Willmoore Kendall in "Prophet of the Heartland," *The World & I,* Feb. 1986, pp. 662-69. The Helms speech was recorded in the *Congressional Record,* volume 129, number 130 (Oct. 3, 1983). Reflections on multiculturalism and the King holiday in "The Cult of Dr. King," *Chronicles,* May 1988, pp. 25-29. The King holiday in perspective in "Why Race Matters," *American Renaissance,* Sept. 1994.

6. AMERICA FIRST. The Francis-Buchanan America First program in "America First," *Chronicles,* Dec. 1991, pp. 4-5. On the conversation with Pat Buchanan, see Samuel T. Francis, "From Household to Nation," *Chronicles,* March 1996, pp. 13-16. The meeting at Buchanan's residence recalled in Gottfried, *Encounters,* pp. 156.

7. A POPULIST REVOLUTION? Culture and power strategy in Samuel T. Francis, "Winning the Culture War," address to the American Cause Foundation, Washington, D.C., May 15, 1993. Printed in *Chronicles* under the same title, December 1993.

8. PURGED. The pithy evaluation of Newt Gingrich in "Gnostic Newt," *Chronicles,* May 1995, pp. 9-10. The explosive lines in Samuel T. Francis, "Why Race Matters," remarks made at the May 1994 American Renaissance conference, published in the Sept. 1994 issue of *American Renaissance.* The defense in Patrick J. Buchanan, "Foreword," in *Shots Fired: Sam Francis on America's Culture War,* p. xii. The critique of the Southern Baptists' apology in "All Those Things to Apologize For," Washington *Times,* June 27, 1995, p. A23. For the dismissal from the *Washington Times,* see Samuel T. Francis, "The Rise and Fall of a Paleoconservative, Part I and II," in *Chronicles,* June 1996, pp. 10-12, and July 1996, pp. 11-13. Hoppe's address reprinted in Hans-Herman Hoppe, *Democracy: The God That Failed* (London: Routledge, 2001), pp. 150-160.

9. CONSERVATIVE WARS. The attempted deforestation of antiwar critics in David Frum, "Unpatriotic Americans," *National Review,* March 25, 2003, pp. 22-26. The patriotic opposition to the Iraq War in Samuel T. Francis, "The Iraq War: Patriotism, True and

False," in *Neo-Conned!: Just War Principles: A Condemnation of War in Iraq*. For the defense of Thomas Jefferson see "Historical Trash Talk," in *New American*, June 26, 1999, pp. 20-23.

10. EXPLICIT. Tackling this lighting rod issue in "The Origins of Racism," *American Renaissance*, May 1999. The dissection of the *Brown vs. Board* decision in "Fifty Years of *Brown* Blunder: Ruling Class Learns Nothing," Creators Syndicate, May 17, 2004.

11. A PEP TALK FOR WESTERN MAN. The case for European peoples in Edwin Clark, "The Roots of the White Man," *American Renaissance*, November and December 1996. "Edwin Clark" is a pseudonym for Samuel T. Francis. According to Jared Taylor, "Francis used the pseudonym "because this [essay] ranges across very broad areas of learning and he may not have wanted to be held strictly to account for his contents."

12. AMERICA SURRENDERED. The eye-opening takes on Sept. 11, 2001, in "Why They Attack Us," Creators Syndicate, Sept. 16, 2001, and "Afterword" in *America Extinguished: Mass Immigration and the Disintegration of American Culture*, pp. 211-215. Columns by Samuel T. Francis from Creators Syndicate on the effects of mass immigration include: "Hate Now Includes All Opposition to Immigration" (Aug. 27, 1999), "Immigration Gives Rise to Ethnic Separatism and Break-Up of U.S." (Feb. 15, 2000), "Immigration Imports Poverty—on Purpose" (Aug. 29, 2000), "Uncontrolled Immigration Brings Uncontrolled Diseases" (Dec, 29, 2000), "Language Anarchy May Fracture Bonds" (June 2, 2000), "Buchanan Broaches Issues No One Else Will Talk About" (Oct. 17, 2000).

13. A PROPHET IS PROVED RIGHT. For Francis's impact on the 2016 election, see Michael Brendan Dougherty, "How An Obscure Adviser to Pat Buchanan Predicted the Wild Trump campaign in 1996," *This Week*, Nov. 12, 2016, pp. 32-35. David Brooks, "The Coming War on Business," *New York Times*, Sept. 22, 2017, p. A24.

14. FRANCIS AT REST. Sam Francis's final essay was "Synthesizing Tyranny," *Chronicles*, April 2005, pp. 10-14. Tributes to Sam Francis in *Chronicles* include those by Thomas Fleming and Clyde Wilson in the May 2005 number and those by Chilton Williamson, Jr., Roger McGrath, Srdja Trifkovic, Vladimir Palko, and Scott P. Richert in the June 2005 number. Joseph Sobran's tribute in "Samuel T. Francis, RIP," *The Wanderer,* Feb. 24, 2005, p. 5. Jared Taylor's tribute in "Sam Francis, RIP," *American Renaissance*, April 2005, p. 1-3. *Washington Times* obituary, "Sam Francis, Columnist, 57, Dies," Feb. 16, 2005, p. 20. *Washington Post* obituary, "Conservative Writer Samuel T. Francis," by Joe Holley, Feb. 26, 2005, p. 20. Buchanan's tribute, "Sam Francis: Obdurate for Truth," *Creators Syndicate*, March 7, 2005.

Acknowledgments

THANKS to the following individuals who answered my queries and supplied information on Sam Francis's life and career: Sam Dickson, Thomas Fleming, Paul Gottfried, Fran Griffin, Louis March, John Shelton Reed, Scott P, Richert, Jared Taylor, Chilton Williamson Jr., Clyde Wilson, and Jerry Woodruff.

On the editing end, thanks to Tom Fleming, Paul Gottfried, Clyde Wilson, and my wife Anna for reading, revising, and offering suggestions as this volume went through several drafts. All mistakes are the author's alone.

Above all, thanks to Mrs. Julia Irwin, sister of Sam Francis, for providing valuable family background.

Bibliography

BOOKS BY SAMUEL T. FRANCIS

The Soviet Strategy of Terror. Washington: Heritage Foundation, 1981. Revised edition, 1985.

Smuggling Revolution: The Sanctuary Movement. Washington: Capital Research Center, 1986.

Power and History, The Political Thought of James Burnham. Lanham, MD: University Press of America, 1984. Republished in 1999 as *James Burnham: Thinkers of Our Time*. London: Claridge Press.

Beautiful Losers: Essays on the Failure of American Conservatism. Columbia: University of Missouri Press, 1993.

Revolution From the Middle. Raleigh: Middle America Press, 1997.

America Extinguished: Mass Immigration and the Disintegration of American Culture. Washington: Americans for Immigration Control, 2001.

Shots Fired: Sam Francis on America's Culture War. Edited by Peter Gemma. Vienna, VA: FGF Books, 2006.

Essential Writings on Race. Vienna VA: New Century Foundation, 2007.

Leviathan And Its Enemies: Mass Organization and Managerial Power in Twentieth Century America. Arlington, VA: Washington Summit Publisher, 2016.

SELECTED ESSAYS BY SAMUEL T. FRANCIS

"Foreign Policy and the South, in Fifteen Southerners, *Why the South Will Survive,* ed. Clyde Wilson. Athens: University of Georgia Press, 1981.

"Message from MARS: The Social Politics of the New Right," in *The New Right Papers.* New York: St. Martin's Press, 1982.

"The Prophet of the Heartland," *World and I,* Feb. 1986.

"The Evil That Men Don't Do: Joe McCarthy and the American Right," *Chronicles,* Sept. 1986.

"The Cult of Dr. King," *Chronicles,* May 1988.

"This Land Ain't Your Land," *Chronicles,* Jan. 1990.

"Beautiful Losers: The Failure of American Conservatives," *Chronicles,* May 1991.

"Equality as a Political Weapon," *Essays in Political Economy: Equality and the Free Society.* Auburn: Ludwig von Mises Institute, July 1991. From a Mises Institute Conference, Princeton, April 13, 1991.

"America First," *Chronicles,* Dec. 1991.

"An Electorate of Sheep," *Chronicles,* Nov. 1992.

"Christians and Republicans," Creators Syndicate, Nov. 27, 1992.

"Culture and Power: Winning the Culture War, *Chronicles.* December 1993. From the American Foundation Conference, Washington, May 15, 1993.

"Anarcho-Tyranny, U.S.A.," *Chronicles,* July 1994.

"Interview with Sam Francis," *Southern Partisan,* Spring 1995.

"From Household to Nation: The Middle American Populism of Pat Buchanan," *Chronicles,* March 1996.

Bibliography

"The Roots of the White Man," *American Renaissance,* November/December 1996.

"New Study Shows Immigration Threatens Democracy," Creators Syndicate, Oct. 16, 1998.

"Homosexual Prejudices of Psychoanalysts," Creators Syndicate, Jan. 1, 1999.

"Immigration Control Must Come from the Grass Roots," Creators Syndicate, Jan. 5, 1999.

"Media Elite Versus Christian Heritage," Creators Syndicate, April 13, 1999.

"Guilt Trip Over the Crusades Is Rejection of the West," Creators Syndicate, April 27, 1999.

"The Origins of Racism," *American Renaissance,* May 1999.

"Lists of Classics Show Political Bias," Creators Syndicate, July 9, 1999.

"FBI Misled Public with Description of Suspect," Creators Syndicate, July 23, 1999.

"Hate Now Includes All Opposition to Immigration," Creators Syndicate, Aug. 27, 1999.

"Immigration Gives Rise to Ethnic Separatism and the Breakup of the United States," Creators Syndicate, Feb. 15, 2000.

"Pope's Apology Endorses Anti-Western 'Culture of Guilt,'" Creators Syndicate, March 17, 2000.

"European-American Month Forfeits Claim to Define Civilization," Creators Syndicate, May 16, 2000.

"Americans Re-Invent Their Own Government in Arizona," Creators Syndicate, June 27, 2000.

"Immigration Imports Poverty—On Purpose," Creators Syndicate, Aug. 29, 2000.

"Immigration Overwhelms Small Towns," Creators Syndicate, Dec. 8, 2000.

"Restore Washington's Birthday," Creators Syndicate, Jan. 28, 2001.

"The Christian Question," *Occidental Quarterly*, Fall 2001.

"The Reagan Legacy—A Mixed Success" Creators Syndicate, June 8, 2004.

"Confronting the Dilemma Conservatives Face," Creators Syndicate, Oct. 22, 2004.

"The War on Christmas is a War on the West," Creators Syndicate, Dec. 14, 2004.

"The Iraq War: Patriotism, True and False," in *Neo-Conned! Just War Principles: A Condemnation of the War in Iraq*, eds. Forrest Sharpe and D. Liam Huallachain. Vienna VA: HIS Press, 2005.

"In Defense of Symbols: Southern and Otherwise," an Address to the Sixth Annual Conference of the Great Revival in the Southern Armies, Harrisonburg VA, July 12, 2000. Printed in *Shots Fired: Sam Francis on America' Culture War*.

Bibliography

SELECTED ESSAYS AND REVIEWS ABOUT SAMUEL T. FRANCIS

Attarian, John. Review of *America Extinguished, Social Contract Press*, Spring 2004, p. 12-15.

Brimelow, Peter. "In Memoriam: Sam Francis," Vdare.com, Feb.16, 2005.

Brooks, David. "The Coming War on Business," *New York Times*, Sept. 27, 2017, p. 25A.

Buchanan, Patrick J. "Sam Francis: Obdurate for Truth," Creators Syndicate, March 7, 2005.

Cavanaugh, Gilbert. "Remembering Sam Francis," *American Renaissance*, Feb. 14, 2015, p. 8.

Daugherty, Michael Brendan. "The Castaway," *America's Future*, Jan. 14, 2007, p. 15-18.

—"How an Obscure Advisor Predicted the Wild Trump Ride," *This Week*, Jan. 19, 2016, pp. 1, 16.

Dickson, Sam. "Sam Francis: An American Hero, Dies," *American Renaissance*, April 2005, pp. 4-6.

Fleming, Thomas. "Requiescat in Pace, Domino," *Chronicles*, April 2024, p. 25.

Genovese, Eugene. "Class, Power, Again: Addressing Samuel Francis," review of *Beautiful Losers* in *Crisis*, Sept. 1, 1994, pp. 25-26.

Gordon, David. "Beyond the Beltway with Burnham," review of *Beautiful Losers* in *Mises Review*, Fall 1995, p. 33.

Gottfried, Paul. "Parallel Lives: William F. Buckley vs. Sam Francis," Vdare.com, Feb. 20, 2005.

—"In Defense of Sam Francis," *Chronicles*, November 2021, p. 6.

Griffin, Fran. "Tribute to Sam Francis," *Sobran's*, February 2000, p. 1.

Himmelfarb, Dan. "Neocon-Bashing," review of *Beautiful Losers* in *Commentary*, Feb. 1994, pp. 50-52.

Hood, Gregory. "Sam Francis, The Prophet," unzreview.com, Sept. 27, 2019.

March, Louis. "Remembering Sam Francis," *Occidental Quarterly*, Summer 2005, p. 10.

Masters, Michael. "The Revolution Within," review of *Shots Fired* in *Social Contract Press*, Spring 2007, pp. 12-14.

Scotchie, Joseph. "Can't Keep a Great Man Down," *Chronicles*, Oct. 2024, pp. 20-23.

Sobran, Joseph. "Sam Francis, RIP," *The Wanderer*, Feb. 24, 2005, p. 1.

— "Francis And His Enemies," *The Wanderer*, March 3, 2005, p. 1.

Taylor, Jared. "Sam Francis, RIP," *American Renaissance*, April 2005, pp. 1-3.

Taylor, Sarah Knox. "Death of A Pilgrim," WTM Enterprises, March 2005, p. 1.

Webster, Stephen. "Sounding The Alarm," review of *America Extinguished* in *American Renaissance*, July 9, 2001, p. 8.

Wilson, Clyde. "A Day with Sam Francis, Willie Pie's Store, Crozier, Virginia, December 26, 1992." In Wilson, *From Union to Empire* (Foundation for American Education, 2003), pp. 297-300.

Index

Albright, Madeline— 8

America Extinguished— 3, 145, 147, 157, 170, 185, 189, 193

America First— v, vii, 5, 13, 16, 21, 37, 39, 56, 69, 72-73, 75, 77, 79, 81, 83, 91, 96, 135, 148, 166, 184, 190

American Cause— 78, 87, 184

American Renaissance— 11, 98-100, 102, 113, 125, 135, 142, 152, 178, 183-186, 191, 193

Arizona Proposition 204—162, 174

Baylor School— 5, 8

Beautiful Losers— v, 3, 48, 53-56, 58-61, 69, 81, 109, 124, 183, 189-190, 193

Bell Curve, 99

Bennett, William J.— 27, 93

Berry, Wendell— 116

Bossi, Umberto— 86

Bradford, M.E.— vii, 2, 11, 15, 17-18, 25-30, 35-36, 42, 55, 60, 67-68, 78, 96-97, 105, 110, 181, 183

Brimelow, Peter— 132, 149, 151, 193

Brooks, David— 36, 61, 101, 120, 163-164, 185, 193

Brown vs. Board of Education— 55, 126

Brown, Jerry— 55, 126-128, 168-169, 185

Buchanan, Patrick— vii, 2, 9, 11, 13, 17-18, 25, 57, 59-61, 71-80, 83, 85, 87, 96-97, 100, 103-107, 110, 117, 119, 123, 127, 129, 132, 135, 143, 148, 150, 163, 171, 179-180, 184-185, 190, 193

Buckley, William F.— 10-11, 24, 27, 32, 45-46, 54-56, 58, 61-62, 72-73, 83, 86, 96, 117, 129, 149-150, 179, 193

Burnham, James— vii, 2-3, 9-10, 25, 45-47, 50-51, 53, 58-59, 119, 124, 142, 171, 177-178, 189, 193

Bush, George H.W. — 13, 39, 59, 81, 85-86, 120, 129, 131, 149, 153

Bush, George W. — 39, 76, 79-80, 82-83, 86, 93, 113, 115-117, 119-120, 124, 140, 153-155, 165, 168-169, 174, 178

California Proposition 187— 60, 93-94, 152-153, 162

Carlson, Tucker— 92, 116, 163

Carolina Conservative Club— 9

Carter, Jimmy— 21, 24, 32, 37, 61, 104, 137, 147

Center for Immigration Studies (CIS)— 150, 158

Chavez, Linda— 97

Check, Christopher— 179

Cheshire, William— 70-71

Christian Coalition (CC)— 85-87, 92, 126, 152

Chronicles— vii, 1-2, 14-16, 19, 55, 61, 71-73, 86, 89, 95, 102-103, 113, 147, 149, 153, 164, 170, 173, 183-184, 186, 190, 193-194

Clinton, Bill— 66, 79-80, 85, 95-96, 110, 116, 120, 152, 156, 164

Commentary— 16-17, 24-25, 97, 149, 167, 194

Council of Conservative Citizens (C of CC)— 11, 87, 125

Critical Race Theory (CRT)—60, 90, 92, 132

Crutchfield, Sylvia— 110, 113

D'Souza, Dinesh—100, 102

Daugherty, Micheal Brendan— 193

Davidson, Donald— 26, 42

Dickson, Sam— 6, 187, 193

Disraeli, Benjamin— 78

Dole, Robert— 61, 85, 96, 103-105, 150

East, John P.— vii, 8, 11, 19, 27-28, 32-33, 35, 58-59, 69, 72, 126, 140, 145, 166, 168, 180

Ellis, Tom— 33, 76, 148

Equality— 25-26, 30-31, 183, 190

Ervin, Sam— 126, 146

Essential Writings on Race— 3, 189

Ethno-Politics— 3

Evans, M. Stanton— 179

Falwell, Jerry— 59, 85, 100, 148

Fanon, Frantz— 64

Faulkner, William— 26, 38, 119

Federation for American Immigration Reform(FAIR)— 150

Feulner, Edwin— 20, 27

Fleming, Thomas— vii, 1-2, 10-11, 13-17, 19, 28, 30, 36, 42, 54-55, 59-60, 71, 75, 86-87, 96-98, 100, 105, 107-109, 114, 116-117, 119, 147-150, 172, 174-175, 179, 183, 186-187, 193

Forbes, Mary Lou— 70, 96, 104-105, 168

Forrest, Nathan Bedford— 87, 92, 176, 192

Frum, David— 117, 184

Gemma, Peter— 60, 189

Genovese, Eugene— 18, 193

Gingrich, Newt— 95-96, 132, 184

Goldberg, Stephen— 30

Goldwater, Barry— 13, 16, 19, 26, 40, 62, 77, 79, 83, 129, 131

Goodlatte, Robert— 154, 165

Gottfried, Paul— 11, 16-17, 43, 53, 55, 61, 71, 78, 107, 110, 123, 179, 184, 187, 193

Gramsci, Antonio— 2, 50, 89

Grant, Bob— 130, 148

Hayek, Fredrich— 106

Helms, Jesse— 11, 27, 33, 35, 62-63, 69, 72, 76, 180, 184

Hemmings, Sally— 66, 114, 130

Heritage Foundation— vii, 11, 14, 19, 23-24, 33, 41, 43, 89, 123, 168, 180, 189

Hoppe, Hans-Hermann — 106-108, 184

Immigration legislation — 44, 146-147, 152, 155, 162, 165

Immigration Reform Caucus (IRC) — 153-154

Index

Irwin, Julia — 6, 187
Israel — 17, 110
Jackson, Andrew — 196
Jaffa, Harry — 25-26, 28
Jefferson, Thomas — 4, 66-68, 90, 92, 105-106, 109, 114-115, 130, 137, 151, 172, 185
John Birch Society — 19, 56, 110
John Randolph Club — 10, 105, 116, 170, 174
Johns Hopkins Institute— 196
Johnson, Lyndon— 12, 37, 55-56, 81
Kauffman, Bill— 116
Kemp, Jack— 93, 95, 100, 150, 165
Kendall, Willmoore— 2, 10, 26, 32, 58-59, 174, 177, 183
Kennedy, Edward— 44, 146
John F. Kennedy —12, 55-56, 81, 146-147
King Jr., Martin Luther— 53, 61-65, 68, 79-80, 124, 129, 181, 184, 190
Kirk, Russell —2, 10, 17-18, 25-26, 32, 50, 69, 78, 109, 119
Kopff, E. Christian— 9-10, 13, 16, 19
Kristol, Irving— 24
Landess, Thomas— 15, 35
Le Pen, Jean Marie— 170-171
League of the South (LOS)— 86-87, 114
Lee, Robert E.— 1, 4, 15, 66-68, 92, 129-131, 137, 166, 172
Limbaugh, Rush— 85, 96, 150, 163
Lincoln, Abraham— 26-27, 66-67, 117, 129-130, 181
Lincoln, Mary Todd— 6

Lott, Trent— 125-126
Lovecraft, H.P.— 2, 9
Lukacs, John— 18
March, Louis— 21, 23, 113, 183, 187, 194
Marcuse, Herman— 18, 64
MARS (Middle American Radicals)— vii, 2, 40-41, 59, 85, 88-89, 94, 119, 135, 167, 174, 190
Marx, Karl—64
Mazzoli, Roman— 152
McCain, John— 80, 115, 153-154, 165, 174
McCarthy, Joseph— 56-58, 61, 151, 183, 190
McConnell, Mitch— 165
McConnell, Scott— 12, 110, 117, 149, 153, 165
McGrath, Roger— 176, 186
Meese, Edwin— 21
Meyer, Frank— 10, 26, 32, 55, 58, 69
Middle American News— 21, 113
Molnar, Thomas— 18
Mosca, Roberto— 50
Moynihan, Daniel P.— 63
Murray, Charles— 2, 5, 11, 17-18, 72, 99, 106, 110, 115
National Association for the Advancement of Colored People (NAACP) — 79, 127
National Endowment for the Arts— 50, 106
National Endowment for the Humanities— 17, 27, 50, 110, 181

National Review (NR)— 9-10, 12, 20, 24-25, 27, 36, 45-46, 54-56, 58, 67, 98-100, 105, 110, 117, 149-150, 153, 167, 177, 184

Nelson, Gaylord— 151-152, 159

Neocon— 16, 25, 27, 115-116, 181, 185, 192 194

New Republic— 46

New Right Papers— 35, 39, 190

New York Post— 110, 149, 153

New York Times— 5, 27, 67, 72, 108, 185, 193

Nixon, Richard M.— vii, 13, 17-19, 40, 55, 58, 66, 77, 81, 129, 131, 133, 148

Numbers USA— 150-151, 162

O'Sullivan, John— 149-150, 153

Obama, Barack— 118

Obergfell Decision—120

Orban, Viktor — 171

Paleoconservative— 16, 117-118, 123, 184

Pareto, Victor—50

Paul, Rand— 39

Percy, Walker—10

Perot, H. Ross—60, 79-80, 96

Phillips, Howard— 82

Phillips, Kevin— 148

Palko, Vladimir— 176, 186

Podhoretz, Norman— 17, 24, 86, 110, 149

Power and History— 3, 45-46, 79, 189

Powell, Enoch— 149

Pruden, Wes— 102, 108

Rahv, Philip— 46

Reagan, Ronald— vii, 11, 13, 16-17, 19-21, 25, 27-28, 32, 39-40, 44-45, 53-54, 57-59, 61-62, 65-66, 77, 79, 82-83, 100-101, 108-109, 120, 129- 131, 133, 152, 170, 181, 192

Reed, John Shelton— 9, 16, 35-36, 85, 183, 187

Reed, Ralph—85

Revolution From the Middle— 151

Richert, Scott P.— 170, 186-187

Robertson, Pat— 59, 86

Rockford Institute— 15, 72, 105, 179

Rockwell, Lew— 106, 116-117

Roe vs. Wade— 82, 119-120

Rothbard, Murray— 2, 11, 17-18, 72, 75, 106, 110

Rusher, William— 35-36, 56, 59

Russell, Richard— 2, 17-18, 25-26, 32, 54, 69, 78, 146, 173

Ryan, Paul— 165

Salvini, Matteo— 87

Scalia, Antonin— 26, 179

Scotchie, Joseph— iii-iv, viii, 10, 73, 98, 108-109, 194

September 11, 2001— iv-v, vii, 2, 5-6, 8-17, 19-28, 30-33, 35-37, 39-40, 43-48, 50, 53-73, 76, 78-83, 85, 87-93, 95-100, 102-106, 108-110, 113-120, 123-124, 126, 129-131, 133, 135-136, 142-152, 154-156, 158-159, 162-165, 167-169, 179, 181, 183-185, 189-194

Shakespeare, William—22, 138

Index

Shots Fired— 3, 184, 189, 192, 194

Smith, Lamar— 21, 35, 152, 155

Smuggling Revolution— 44, 189

Sobran, Joseph— 11, 45, 51, 72, 75, 83, 96, 108, 116, 119, 132, 150, 155, 177, 194

Southern Partisan— 13, 15, 35, 67, 113, 147, 169, 190

Soviet Strategy of Terror— 3, 43, 189

Tancredo, Thomas— 148, 153-154, 174

Taunton, John— 90

Taylor, Jared— 2-3, 11, 98, 102, 132, 135-136, 142-143, 177, 185, 187, 194

Trump, Donald— 4, 13, 60, 66, 92, 103-104, 132, 163-167, 171, 185, 193

University of Missouri Press— 53, 60, 189

University of North Carolina— vii, 9, 180

Unz, Ron— 113, 194

Vdare.com— 193

Viguerie, Richard— 82

Voegelin, Eric— 32

Von Mises Institute 183

Wall Street Journal— 5, 55, 105, 149, 167

Wallace, George— 27, 40, 59, 126, 148

Warren, Donald— 2, 26, 36, 40, 148

Washington Times— vii, 2-3, 11-12, 17, 43, 70-71, 86, 98, 102, 113, 139, 158, 163, 167-168, 180, 184, 186

Washington, George— 4, 17, 66, 96, 129, 151

Weaver, Richard M.— 9-10, 30, 32, 50, 69, 119, 137, 170, 203

Why the South Will Survive— 35-36, 183, 190

Williamson, Chilton— 11-12, 17, 45, 51, 55, 99, 119, 147-148, 151, 176, 186-187

Wilson, Clyde— 1, 4, 6, 8-9, 11, 13-17, 19, 25, 36-37, 42, 60, 67-68, 70, 86-87, 93-94, 107-108, 119, 148, 176, 181, 183, 186-187, 190, 194

Woodruff, Jerry— 21, 24, 183, 187

Woods, Thomas E.— 108

About the Author

JOSEPH SCOTCHIE has worked as a journalist in the New York City area for over three decades. His work has won a New York State Press Association award and, on two occasions, the North Carolina Society of Historians award. Scotchie's past publications include *The Vision of Richard Weaver, Barbarians in the Saddle: An Intellectual Biography of Richard M. Weaver, The Paleoconservatives, Thomas Wolfe Revisited, Revolt from the Heartland: The Struggle for an Authentic Conservatism, Street Corner Conservatism: Patrick J. Buchanan and His Times, A Gallery of Ashevillians, Writing on the Southern Front: Authentic Conservatism for Our Time,* and *The Asheville Connection.*

Best Sellers and New Releases

Over 90 Titles For You To Enjoy

SHOTWELLPUBLISHING.COM

THE SOUTH'S FINEST CONTEMPORARY AUTHORS.

Shotwell Publishing is proud to be called home by many of today's most respected Southern scholars and literary greats.

JEFFERY ADDICOTT
Union Terror: Debunking the False Justifications for Union Terror

Trampling Union Terror: Riders of the Second Alabama Cavalry

MARK ATKINS
Women in Combat: Feminism Goes to War

JOYCE BENNETT
Maryland, My Maryland: The Cultural Cleansing of a Small Southern State

GARRY BOWERS
Slavery and The Civil War: What Your History Teacher Didn't Tell You

Dixie Days: Reminiscences Of a Southern Boyhood

JERRY BREWER
Dismantling the Republic

ANDREW P. CALHOUN
My Own Darling Wife: Letters From A Confederate Volunteer

JOHN CHODES
Segregation: Federal Policy or Racism?

Washington's KKK: The Union League During Southern Reconstruction

WALTER BRIAN CISCO
War Crimes Against Southern Civilians

DAVID T. CRUM
Stonewall Jackson: Saved by Providence

JOHN DEVANNY
Continuities: The South in a Time of Revolution

Lincoln's Continuing Revolution: Essays of M.E. Bradford and Thomas H. Landess

JOSHUA DOGGRELL
Doxed: The Political Lynching of a Southern Cop

JAMES C. EDWARDS
What Really Happened?: Quantrill's Raid On Lawrence, Kansas

TED EHMANN
Boom & Bust In Bone Valley: Florida's Phosphate Mining History 1886-2021

JOHN AVERY EMISON
The Deep State Assassination of Martin Luther King Jr.

DON GORDON
Snowball's Chance: My Kidneys Failed, My Wife Left Me & My Dog Died...

JOHN R. GRAHAM
Constitutional History of Secession

PAUL C. GRAHAM
Confederaphobia

When The Yankees Come: Former Carolina Slaves Remember

Nonsense on Stilts: The Gettysburg Address & Lincoln's Imaginary Nation

JOE D. HAINES
The Diary of Col. John Henry Stover Funk of the Stonewall Brigade, 1861-1862

CHARLES HAYES
The REAL First Thanksgiving

V.P. HUGHES
Col. John Singleton Mosby: In the News 1862-1916

TERRY HULSEY
25 Texas Heroes

The Constitution of Non-State Government: Field Guide to Texas Secession

JOSEPH JAY
Sacred Conviction: The South's Stand for Biblical Authority

JAMES R. KENNEDY
Dixie Rising: Rules For Rebels

Nullifying Federal and State Gun Control: A How-To Guide For Gun Owners

When Rebel Was Cool: Growing Up In Dixie, 1950-1965

Reconstruction: Destroying the Republic and Creating an Empire

WALTER D. KENNEDY
The South's Struggle: America's Hope

Lincoln, The Non-Christian President: Exposing The Myth

Lincoln, Marx, and the GOP

J.R. & W.D. KENNEDY
Jefferson Davis: High Road to Emancipation and Constitutional Government

Yankee Empire: Aggressive Abroad and Despotic at Home

Punished With Poverty: The Suffering South

The South Was Right! 3rd Edition

LEWIS LIBERMAN
Snowflake Buddies; ABC Leftism For Kids!

PHILIP LEIGH
The Devil's Town: Hot Springs During The Gangster Era

U.S. Grant's Failed Presidency

The Causes of the Civil War

The Dreadful Frauds: Critical Race Theory And Identity Politics

JACK MARQUARDT
Around The World In 80 Years: Confessions of a Connecticut Confederate

MICHAEL MARTIN
Southern Grit: Sensing The Siege at Petersburg

SAMUEL MITCHAM
The Greatest Lynching In American History: New York, 1863

Confederate Patton: Richard Taylor and The Red River Campaign

CHARLES T. PACE
Lincoln As He Really Was

Southern Independence. Why War? The War To Prevent Southern Independence

JAMES R. ROESCH
From Founding Fathers To Fire Eaters

KIRKPATRICK SALE
Emancipation Hell: The Tragedy Wrought By Lincoln's Emancipation Proclamation

JOSEPH SCOTCHIE
The Asheville Connection: The Making of a Conservative

ANNE W. SMITH
Charlottesville Untold: Inside Unite The Right

Robert E. Lee: A History for Kids

KAREN STOKES
A Legion Of Devils: Sherman In South Carolina

The Burning of Columbia, S.C.: A Review of Northern Assertions and Southern Facts

Carolina Love Letters

Fortunes of War: The Adventures of a German Confederate

A Confederate in Paris: Letters of A. Dudley Mann 1867-1879

JOSEPH R. STROMBERG
Southern Story and Song: Country Music in the 20th Century

JACK TROTTER
Last Train to Dixie

JOHN THEURSAM
Key West's Civil War

H.V. TRAYWICK, JR.
Along The Shadow Line: A Road Trip through History and Memory on the Old Confederate Border

LESLIE TUCKER
Old Times There Should Not Be Forgotten: Cultural Genocide In Dixie

JOHN VINSON
Southerner Take Your Stand!

MARK R. WINCHELL
Confessions of a Copperhead: Culture and Politics in the Modern South

CLYDE N. WILSON
Calhoun: A Statesman for the 21st Century

Lies My Teacher Told Me: The True History of the War For Southern Independence

The Yankee Problem: An American Dilemma

Annals Of The Stupid Party: Republicans Before Trump

Nullification: Reclaiming The Consent of the Governed

The Old South: 50 Essential Books

The War Between The States: 60 Essential Books

Reconstruction and the New South, 1865-1913: 50 Essential Books

The South 20th Century And Beyond: 50 Essential Books

Southern Poets and Poems, 1606-1860: The Land They Loved, Volume 1

Confederate Poets and Poems, Vol1 The Land They Loved, Volume II

Looking For Mr. Jefferson

African American Slavery in Historical Perspective

JOE WOLVERTON
What Degree Of Madness?: Madison's Method To Make American States Again

WALTER KIRK WOOD
Beyond Slavery: The Northern Romantic Nationalist Origins of America's Civil War

SHOTWELLPUBLISHING.COM

Green Altar (Literary Imprint)

CATHARINE SAVAGE BROSMAN
*An Aesthetic Education
and Other Stories (2nd Ed)*

Chained Tree, Chained Owls: Poems

Aerosols and Other Poems

Partial Memoirs

RANDALL IVEY
*A New England Romance:
And Other Southern Stories*

The Gift of Gab

SUZANNE JOHNSON
Maxcy Gregg's Sporting Journals 1842-1858

JAMES E. KIBLER, JR.
Tiller : Claybank County Series, Vol. 4

The Gentler Gamester

*In the Deep Heart's Core: Poems of Tribute and
Remembrance (forthcoming)*

THOMAS MOORE
*A Fatal Mercy:
The Man Who Lost The Civil War*

PERRIN LOVETT
The Substitute, Tom Ironsides 1

KAREN STOKES
Belles

Carolina Twilight

Honor in the Dust

The Immortals

The Soldier's Ghost: A Tale of Charleston

WILLIAM THOMAS
*Runaway Haley:
An Imagined Family Saga*

*The Field of Justice: Moonshine
and Murder in North Georgia*

CLYDE N. WILSON
*Southern Poets and Poems, 1606-1860:
The Land They Loved, Volume 1*

*Confederate Poets and Poems, Vol 1
The Land They Loved, Volume II*

Gold-Bug
(Mystery & Suspense Imprint)

BRANDI PERRY
Splintered: A New Orleans Tale

MARTIN WILSON
To Jekyll and Hide

Free Book Offer

DON'T GET LEFT OUT, Y'ALL.
Sign-up and be the first to know about new releases, sales, and other goodies
—plus we'll send you TWO FREE EBOOKS!

Lies My Teacher Told Me:
The True History of the War for
Southern Independence
by Dr. Clyde N. Wilson

When The Yankees Come
Former Carolina Slaves Remember
Sherman's March From the Sea
by Paul C. Graham

FreeLiesBook.com

Southern Books. No Apologies.
We love the South — its history,
traditions, and culture — and are proud
of our inheritance as Southerners.
Our books are a reflection of this love.

www.ingramcontent.com/pod-product-compliance
Lightning Source LLC
Chambersburg PA
CBHW070550160426
43199CB00014B/2442